IRISH CHURCHES AND MONASTERIES

AN HISTORICAL AND ARCHITECTURAL GUIDE

D0255044

IRISH CHURCHES AND MONASTERIES
AN HISTORICAL AND ARCHITECTURAL GUIDE

Seán D. O'Reilly

THE COLLINS PRESS

Published by The Collins Press, Carey's Lane, The Huguenot
Quarter, Cork 1997

Printed in Ireland by Colour Books Ltd., Dublin

Jacket design by Upper Case Ltd., Cornmarket Street, Cork

ISBN: 1-898256-14-4

For Anne

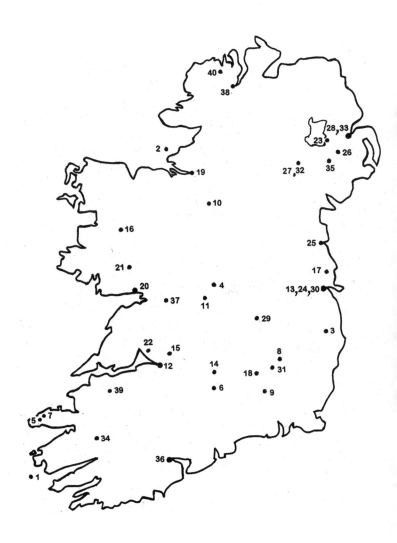

LOCATION MAP

1. Skellig Michael, County Kerry
2. Innishmurray Island, County Sligo
3. Glendalough, County Wicklow
4. Clonmacnois, County Offaly
5. Gallarus Oratory, County Kerry
6. Cormac's Chapel, Cashel
7. Kilmalkedar Church, County Kerry
8. St Laserian's Cathedral, Old Leighlin
9. Jerpoint Abbey, County Kilkenny
10. Boyle Abbey, County Roscommon
11. Clonfert Cathedral, County Galway
12. St Mary's Cathedral, Limerick
13. Christ Church Cathedral, Dublin
14. Holy Cross Abbey, County Tipperary
15. St Flannan's Cathedral, Killaloe
16. Ballintubber Abbey, County Mayo
17. St Doulagh's Church, County Dublin
18. St Canice's Cathedral, Kilkenny
19. Sligo Abbey, Sligo
20. St Nicholas of Myra, Galway
21. Ross Errilly Friary, Headford
22. Quin Abbey, County Clare
23. Ballinderry Church, County Antrim
24. St Michan's Church, Dublin
25. St Peter's Church, Drogheda
26. St Malachy's Church, Hillsborough
27. Primate Robinson's Chapel, Armagh
28. First Presbyterian Church, Belfast
29. St John the Evangelist, Coolbanagher
30. St Mary's Pro-Cathedral, Dublin
31. St John's Church, Shankill
32. St Patrick's Cathedral, Armagh
33. St Malachy's Church, Belfast
34. St Mary's Cathedral, Killarney
35. First Presbyterian Church, Banbridge
36. St Fin Barre's Cathedral, Cork
37. St Brendan's Cathedral, Loughrea
38. St Eunan's Cathedral, Letterkenny
39. Knockanure Church, Moyvane
40. St Michael's Church, Creeslough

ACKNOWLEDGEMENTS

The author would like to thank sincerely all those who helped in any way towards the completion of the book.

Thanks are due to Faber and Faber Ltd. for permission to reproduce the extract from Séamus Heaney's poem 'In Gallarus Oratory' from *Door into the Dark*.

Photography is by Anne O'Reilly except for the following where the permission to use is much appreciated.

Interior of First Presbyterian Church, Rosemary Street, Belfast, courtesy of Tom Moore.

Photograph of mummified bodies in St Michan's Church, Dublin by courtesy of the Christ Church Cathedral Group of Parishes.

Department of Arts, Culture and the Gaeltacht for permission to reproduce the photographs on pages 16, 27, 33, 42, 44, 65, 71, 73 and 105.

CONTENTS

INTRODUCTION

Although there is evidence of Christian teaching in Ireland before his time, credit for the conversion of this Celtic island to Christianity goes mainly to the fifth-century St Patrick, who before his death had already set the seeds of both an episcopal and monastic system for Ireland. It was the monastic system that first took deepest root. The early monastic establishments were places of retreat from the world, often set up in remote parts and on islands off the west coast – small, self-governing groups of monks sharing a community life of service to God. In these monastic centres, wherever timber was plentiful, the wattle-and-daub huts of the monks were grouped around one or more wooden churches of rectangular shape. Of course, no trace of any of these remains today. Among the earliest Irish churches surviving in whole or in part are the few rectangular drystone corbel-built oratories found in the Dingle Peninsula and on the western island of Skellig Michael. Growth and prestige soon transformed a handful of mainland foundations like Glendalough and Clonmacnois into monastic cities, and promoters of a great religious, literary, and artistic culture. It was indeed a Golden Age for Ireland.

Monasteries were key targets in the Viking raids of the ninth and tenth centuries. These raids gave a new impetus to building in stone. Typical early stone churches – many still lying in ruins across the landscape – were small, single-chambered, rectangular structures with mortared walls and roofs of wooden shingles or thatch.

The term Romanesque, which occupies the Irish architectural stage from about 1120, applies rather to a new art style than to structural changes. With one or two notable exceptions, churches continued to be built in the older manner, with Irish Romanesque leaving its imprint on doorways, windows, and chancel arches in a riot of decorative motifs – chevrons, frets, scallops, interlacings, human and animal heads, and stylised foliage designs.

11

With the advent of the Cistercian monks in 1142 came the first abbeys and the final eclipse of the old monastic system of scattered huts and oratories. Church Synods at Rathbreasail (1111) and Kells (1152) reorganised the Irish Church along episcopal lines with thirty-six bishoprics, and four archbishoprics at Armagh, Dublin, Cashel, and Tuam. The Anglo-Norman conquest commencing in 1169 added a new generation of churchmen dedicated to the building of abbeys and cathedrals, and of large parish churches in the new Anglo-Norman towns. After a short Transitional period lasting from about 1160 to 1200, during which it was often blended with Romanesque forms, Irish Gothic developed. It adopted in turn the forms of thirteenth-century Early English and fourteenth-century Decorated Gothic, but the characteristically pointed arches, clustered columns, lancet and traceried windows and rib-vaulted ceilings were always subject to unexpected Irish twists.

Church building everywhere was brought to a long halt by the Black Death that swept across from Asia and Europe in the mid-fourteenth century, but the fifteenth century saw a remarkable resurgence of building activity which included up to forty new Franciscan friaries and restoration of some larger, earlier monasteries. It was a short-lived prosperity, however, because in 1537 Henry VIII began the dissolution of the Irish monasteries, many of which then fell into lay hands, and a new minority Protestant Church of Ireland was given possession of all other church property. There was much damage to existing churches and only a modicum of new building during the troubled Tudor regime that ended with the death of Elizabeth I in 1603. In Irish building there was a modest nineteenth-century Tudor Revival.

The Ulster Plantation of the first decade of the seventeenth century created a predominantly Protestant province, but continued religious and political unrest throughout the century was not conducive to much church building by any denomination.

The eighteenth century began with severe Penal Laws that followed the Catholic defeat at the Battle of the Boyne in

1690. A Protestant Ascendancy was established, followed by a century-long building programme of Protestant churches. Classical style using Palladian or Italian Renaissance models was the norm. After the mid-century a movement in architecture, identified by the term neo-classicism, sought to rediscover the architecture of Greece and Rome by a direct re-examination of the buildings of classical antiquity, and not filtered through the Italian Renaissance. This neo-classical movement lasted from about 1760 to 1850 with Greek Revival predominating as it proceeded. Also after the mid-eighteenth century a second form of reaction against the discredited old classical manner took the form of a Gothic Revival, now identified by its eighteenth-century spelling Gothick, with the *k*. Throughout most of the century, and carrying over until about 1830, the main burden of Church of Ireland building was borne by a Board of First Fruits established in 1711. This Board accounted for the building of about 700 parish churches, where restraints on cost and size admitted for the most part only a discreet Gothic style.

The Penal Laws were well revoked before the turn of the nineteenth century, and the Catholic Emancipation Act of 1829 heralded the resumption of Catholic church building. By the end of the century, new building included several imposing cathedrals that favoured neo-Gothic style. Meanwhile, the Church of Ireland, which still held most of the old historic sites, was suffering from over-endowment and under-attendance. A Church Temporalities Act of 1833, which reduced the number of high church positions, failed to halt the decline, and the Church of Ireland was finally disestablished in 1869. All too frequently bedevilled by small and dwindling congregations, it has continued to survive at various levels of prosperity depending on location.

At the turn of this century a Celtic Revival brought the work of Irish artists into the church scene, but attempts at a renaissance of Irish Romanesque architecture were generally unsuccessful.

The liturgy stipulations of the Second Vatican Council (1962-5) resulted in sanctuary alterations to all Catholic churches, some radical. Across the Irish town and country scene today are many new parish churches that since the 1960s have combined a modern idiom with the requirements of the new liturgy.

Using representative examples, this general reader introduction is intended as a doorway to the world of Irish ecclesiastical architecture, just wide enough to furnish an outline historical, architectural, and descriptive summary. The forty venues selected are arranged chronologically where the dates given mean a *beginning* of building, but the reader will appreciate that much subsequent alteration or restoration was undertaken.

SKELLIG MICHAEL EARLY MONASTERY
Great Skellig, County Kerry

> The scene is one so solemn and so sad that none should enter
> here but the pilgrim and the penitent. The sense of solitude, the
> vast heaven above and the sublime monotonous motion of the
> sea beneath would oppress the spirit, were not that spirit
> brought into harmony ...

This is how Lord Dunraven in 1875 was moved by the
timeless quality of the monastery of Skellig Michael. Yet every
visitor to this extraordinary place is moved in his or her own
particular way, because the whole Skellig experience, from
mainland to rocky eminence, is emotionally and physically in
a class apart.

The 'scene' to which Lord Dunraven referred is a small
cluster of buildings consisting of five clocháns, commonly
called beehive huts, two rectangular stone oratories and a
small ruined ninth-century medieval church, all perched
together some 600 feet (180 metres) above the sea close to the
summit of the Great Skellig, the larger of two islands that rise
jaggedly out of the Atlantic Ocean about 8 miles (13km) to the
west of the Kerry mainland. It was part of the monastic
movement initiated by St Patrick which sent groups of
hermits to places of retreat from the world – and what more
ideal places than the many islands off the west coast of
Ireland? That these monks followed some kind of common
Rule is indicated by annalistic references to the deaths of
several abbots of Skellig Michael between 800 and 1100. The
Annals also record that the monastery was sacked at least four
times during ninth-century Viking raids. Entries are terse, and
telling: '823AD: Skellig was plundered by the heathen, and
Etgal was carried off into captivity, and he died of hunger and
thirst ...' The final entry on the Rock is from the *Annals of the
Four Masters*, dated 1044, which says without elaboration:

Skellig Michael

'Aodh of Skellig Michael died.'

The monks of Skellig Michael retired to the mainland before the end of the twelfth century, after which the Rock came under the jurisdiction of the Augustinians, and became a place of pilgrimage. Visits were made to the cells and chapels, prayer stations being marked by stone crosses, the whole penitential exercise ending in a terrifying ascent to the western summit through a tiny aperture known as the Eye of the Needle, and out along a treacherous narrow spit suspended high above the ocean.

A ninety minute sea journey brings the visitor to the landing stage at Blind Man's Cove, a good period during which to give thought to the sturdy monks as they too plied these waves back and forth in their small skin-covered boats. There is a walk along the lighthouse road to where the climb begins. And what a climb it is! – a stairway of some 600 steps that weaves its way upwards, with some dizzying moments, to reach the monastic enclosure at the summit. Here the

Clocháns on Skellig Michael

visitor comes upon the near-perfect exemplar of the earliest Irish monastic plan, with the individual huts of the monks grouped about the church, and all enclosed within a protective wall of stones.

The clocháns are circular drystone structures built using the corbelling technique. A corbel vault is formed out of a succession of circular courses of flat stones set one above the other, each successive course projecting inwards a little from the one below it to form a load-bearing ledge for the next course. The wall then narrows as it rises, creating a dome-like shelter resembling a beehive. The first clochán reached on the south side is also the largest; it is square on the inside with vertical walls merging into the curve of the exterior wall at a height of about six feet, making it just like an ordinary room with domed ceiling. About the same distance above floor level, the wall is ringed by protruding stone corbels that must have supported an upper wooden floor lighted by a small aperture in the east wall. Protruding stones whose purpose remains open to conjecture are also staggered about the exterior wall. In the manner of some early Irish churches the

17

low doorway is double-lintelled, with the upper lintel designed to carry some of the wall weight.

The two oratories are rectangular in plan, boat-shaped in appearance, the larger one lying close to the huts. Only the east window and portions of the east and adjacent walls remain of the ninth-century church of St Michael, patron saint of high places.

How did a little community of ten to twenty monks manage to eke out an existence on this inhospitable island perch? The island itself provided water, fowl, and seafood. Sea birds and their eggs were plentiful, and fish were caught using hooks, fish-spears and nets. There is a small amount of arable land that would have functioned as a monastic garden, producing common vegetables like peas, parsnips, carrots, and celery. And some of the island's wild plants were also edible. From the mainland came cereal supplies, sheep and goats for meat or grazing, fuel supplies of turf and wood, and even some stones for building. Everything begins to sound comfortable enough if one forgets the ferocity of unpredictable Atlantic gales, and those stretches of bleak winter during which the monks of Skellig Michael must have found themselves marooned in conditions of fearsome isolation.

Location: About 8m (13km) off Kerry mainland. Boats from Portmagee – 12m (19km).

INISHMURRAY ISLAND MONASTERY
Inishmurray Island, County Sligo

Inishmurray is a small island approximately one mile long situated about 4 miles (6.5km) from the nearest mainland point. It is named after some Muiredach (mwir-eh-dock, anglicised to Murray) long passed into oblivion beside Molaise (muh-lash'), who founded here an early sixth-century monastery. However, earliest surviving monastic remains may not be earlier than eighth century, and other building is later. One Viking raid was reported in the *Annals of the Four Masters*: 'AD802 – Inish Muiredach was burned by the foreigners, when they attacked Ros Commain.' This is the only annalistic reference to Innismurray, and leaves the subsequent monastic history wide open to conjecture. Did the monks remain on the island, or did they retire to the mainland monastery of Aughris, also founded by St Molaise? Whatever the picture, Inishmurray thereafter appears to have remained untouched by outside destructive forces, leaving it as it is today as close as one could realistically hope to come to a genuine experience of a typical early Irish monastic settlement.

These ancient settlements generally consisted of a small scattering of buildings enclosed by a wall of earth or stone. In the case of Inishmurray, the roughly oval-shaped drystone cashel wall at once provided shelter and protection, and symbolised the exclusion of the outside world. Whether or not this cashel wall pre-dated the monastery is not known with certainty. With its terraces of steps to the wall top, its souterrains, its chambers built into the thickness of the wall, it quite resembles an Iron Age hillfort of the type of Staigue Fort in County Kerry. Would a group of humble monks have been capable of mustering the labour force required to build such a massive rampart?

Within the confines of this cashel wall the monks

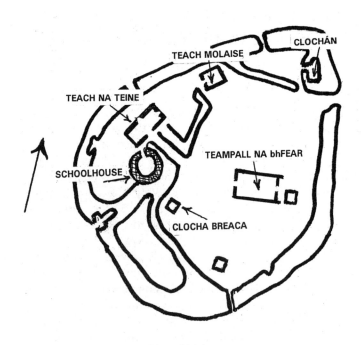

Plan of Inishmurray

followed the prescriptions of a common Rule in obedience to an abbot; from the island itself they found subsistence by farming and fishing. Besides the ruins themselves, tangible remains of the industry of the monks are found in the many cross-inscribed slabs scattered across the island, and later used as prayer stations by pilgrims.

Inishmurray has four identifiable inner enclosures. Undoubtedly, the largest of these was the monastic reserve proper, the rest being used for domestic purposes. Visitors to Reask in the Dingle Peninsula will observe the foundations of a similar arrangement. In the largest enclosure at Inishmurray stands Teampall na bhFear (tchowmpul nuh var), the Church of the Men, also known as Teampall Molaise. In the early and medieval Irish monastic context a church building is frequently called a teampall, meaning a temple. Now roofless,

Schoolhouse, Teach na Teine, Teach Molaise

Teampall Molaise retains the antae and lintelled doorway characteristic of early Irish stone churches. Clearly this was the main monastic church; its other name derives from the fact that men only were buried in its vicinity. Among the many island traditions is one that St Molaise was aided by St Columba (Colmcille) in the building of this Church. When differences arose, St Columba withdrew, but not before he had ordained that men only be interred within the cashel wall.

In the north-western corner of the enclosure containing Teampall na bhFear is the ancient Teach Molaise, Molaise's House, romantically believed to have been the church or cell of the monastic founder. Its stone roof was reconstructed late in the nineteenth century. The low doorway has sloping jambs and a Greek cross is inscribed on the lintel. Tradition has it that Teach Molaise became the tomb-shrine of the founding saint. A thirteenth-century wooden statue of St Molaise formerly kept here is now preserved in the National Museum of Ireland in Dublin. In the matter of dating, Teach Molaise may be as early as eighth century, with Teampall na bhFear making a later appearance.

Spaced about the open area surrounding Teampall na bhFear are three square 'altars' made up of courses of flat stones. These marked three of the Stations, or stopping points, on the pilgrimage rounds of the island that succeeded the demise of the monastery. The top of the Big Station close to the Church is covered with rounded stones probably collected from the seashore. These inoffensive stones, some actually scratched with crosses, are said to have been used as cursing stones by angry islanders wishing to settle enemy scores. The cursing procedure involved circling the Station from right to left, during which the stones were turned over three times, and the curse invoked. There was a catch: if the intended victim was innocent the curse was said to rebound on the instigator! Less menacingly, these stones were given the name Clocha Breaca (kluka braka), or Speckled Stones, but even this harmless title did not deliver them from an alleged property that their correct number could not be counted – meaning that for visual counting, successive attempts would always give different results.

In the west side enclosure are two further buildings. The unroofed rectangular one is known as Teach na Teine (tock nuh tih-neh), the House of the Fire, an unusual name deriving from the fact that it had a central hearth, whose outline remains. Miraculous properties were attributed to this fire: if it were extinguished, spontaneous combustion would occur by the simple expedient of throwing on a sod of turf. And on one occasion the flame was said to have leaped up and consumed a person attempting to desecrate the hearth! It was inevitable that strange beliefs should grow up around Inishmurray. The truth about Teach na Teine is that its conjectured fourteenth-century date of construction puts it later than the monastic occupation, but it *may* occupy the site of the original monastic kitchen.

The other building is one of two beehive huts found within the monastic enclosure. In one version it is called the Schoolhouse, because the low stone seat along its interior wall resembles a school bench. In a radically different version it is

Clocha Breaca and Teampall na bhFear

called Túr Uí Bhrennell (toor ee vrenel), the Waking Place of the Virgins. In the heyday of the monastery, clocháns, or beehive huts, constituted the shelters of the monks, and in the case of Inishmurray there must have been more than the two remaining. The monastic picture can be mentally completed by adding one or two more functional or domestic buildings, either of wood or stone. Not surprisingly for a remote ocean-island, Inishmurray is not graced with a Round Tower, but it would have been nice. Off-shore Round Towers are not unknown, of course; one remains on Devenish Island in Lower Lough Erne, and another on Inishcaltra in Lough Derg. That on Scattery Island took advantage of the shelter of the Shannon Estuary. Undoubtedly, a Round Tower on Inishmurray would have been just too adventurous.

Location: 4m (6.5km) off Sligo mainland. Boats from Mullaghmore and Rosses Point.

23

GLENDALOUGH
County Wicklow

Sheltered by steep, heavily-wooded mountain slopes, the beautifully sequestered vale of Glendalough is the site of the scattered remains of the great monastic city that grew out of the sixth-century hermitage of St Kevin. For all their ruinous condition, these historic monuments continue to exert a magnetic attraction on the thousands of visitors who come each year to view the Seven Churches of Glendalough.

When St Kevin arrived at Glendalough, he *may* have set up a monastery in the area where the Round Tower now stands, and then withdrawn to the solitude of Kevin's Hermitage on the south shore of the Upper Lake, its location marked by the cave known as St Kevin's Bed, and the nearby Temple na Skellig (Church of the Rock). He may also have involved himself in the development of the monastic settlement east of the Lower Lake, where the monastic city of Glendalough grew and flourished in the centuries following the death of its saintly founder.

The ruins that are left are mainly those of the churches. Only the imagination can recreate the many other buildings that once made up the city – the wattle-and-daub and stone beehive huts of the monks, the kitchens and refectories, workshops for carpenter and metalworker, the dairy, mill and bakery, scriptorium, and hospitality house.

In 1111, an historical synod of clergy and laity was convened at Rathbreasail, County Tipperary. It divided Ireland into twenty-two (or twenty-four) territorial sees under archbishoprics at Armagh and Cashel. Henceforth, a hierarchy of archbishop and bishop was to take precedence over the position of abbot in the sphere of Irish Church life. At this Synod, Glendalough was included as one of five bishoprics of Leinster, and embraced the territory of Dublin. One hundred years later, in 1213, the roles were reversed and

Glendalough was annexed to Dublin, which was now under rival Anglo-Norman control. This change marked the beginning of the end for Glendalough. Long before this, however, Glendalough had suffered from frequent plunderings and burnings by Viking marauders. It had survived these misfortunes by quick replacement of wooden structures – an ongoing saga of destruction and renewal, ending in the final devastation of 1398 when the English forces of Richard II brought it to its present state of ruin. Pilgrimages to Glendalough then became the tradition, but by the nineteenth century these 'patterns' had so degenerated into exhibitions of drunkenness and faction fighting that, in 1862, they were finally suppressed by the Church.

The gateway to Glendalough is the only surviving example of an entrance to an early Irish monastery. To the right stands the Cathedral, the largest of the monuments, its west doorway facing the Round Tower. The nave, widest of any early Irish church, probably dates to the ninth century. It has all the usual characteristics of an early Irish stone church – lintelled doorway, projecting antae, small round-arched windows with inclined jambs in the south wall, and none in the north wall. The lower parts of the walls have a rubble core faced with large thin slabs of mica-schist laid on edge; the upper parts are built in uncoursed rubble of smaller stones. There is evidence of rebuilding, doubtless following one or more of the plunderings. The lintelled doorway on the west side is also of mica-schist, the local stone; it has a semi-circular relieving arch above the lintel designed to divert some of the wall weight. Romanesque carvings on the east window and chancel arch date the chancel to mid-twelfth century, or later. Credit for this work is given to St Laurence O'Toole, later Archbishop and now patron saint of Dublin, who was abbot of Glendalough from 1153 to 1162. A portion of the three-order chancel arch reconstructed in the 1870s exhibits some characteristic motifs of Romanesque ornamentation: scalloped capitals, roll mouldings, and zigzags. The addition of chancels to existing churches was a significant structural development in Irish church building that accompanied the reforming Synods of Rathbreasail and Kells; it gave added prestige to the clergy in the newly organised parochial system.

Thatch of marsh reed was the likely roof covering material or, if time and expense were not critical, oak shingles might have been preferred, laid in overlapping courses on top of a boarded-over roof.

Close to the Cathedral for ease of access, and among the finest of its kind in Ireland, is the Round Tower that soars majestically to a height of 103 feet (31.4 metres). Its fallen conical cap was replaced in 1876. The walls are of mica-schist and the round-headed doorway is of granite. Under the cap are four windows facing the cardinal points, and below that one window to each of the five storeys. Those tall freestanding structures called Round Towers are always located within early Irish monastic grounds. In the peaceful sanctuary of the monks a monument like a church steeple pointing up to Heaven was an inspiring symbol. Round Towers were also used as belfries, lookout towers, landmarks for pilgrims, places of protection for monastic valuables, and temporary places of refuge in times of attack. In this latter capacity, an off-the-ground doorway was a necessary security device.

To the south of the Cathedral is St Kevin's Church. It would be a nice romance to think of this tiny oratory as just that – as many have done, and perhaps still do. Its earliest form, however, hardly pre-dates the ninth century. One argument in favour of this dating is its similarity to St Columba's Oratory in Kells, County Meath, which is tied to the ninth-century homecoming of Columban monks from Iona in Scotland. St Columba's Oratory is called a House and, because its quaint belfry tower resembles a chimney, St Kevin's Church is called a Kitchen. Of much more architectural significance is the steeply pitched stone roof built on the corbel principle, and reinforced against inward collapse by an interior pointed barrel-vaulted propping arch. A tiny croft running the length of the roof just below the ridge removes part of the downward load. The wooden floor that

St Kevin's Church

formed at once the ceiling of the church and the floor of an upper attic room has long disappeared. A chancel and sacristy were later additions, the east wall of the Church being opened to form the chancel arch, but the chancel disappeared about 200 years ago, and the exposed chancel arch then became the present doorway of the church. Foundations of the chancel remain clearly visible, also the roof line marked by the inverted V-shape on the east gable of the church. Over the original west doorway is a relieving arch similar to that over the lintel of the Cathedral doorway. Of similar construction to St Kevin's is the Oratory of St Flannan in Killaloe, County Clare.

At Reefert Church the nave and chancel are built in one. For anyone wishing to experience the charm and atmosphere of an early Irish stone church Reefert must be the perfect choice, and its idyllic setting provides an added delight. Unadorned simplicity is the keynote. The doorway has an elemental aspect, its inclined jambs and massive covering

Reefert Church Doorway

lintel formed of well-dressed granite blocks. Later chancel arches of the twelfth-century Irish Romanesque were treated to lavish ornamentation, but at Reefert the undecorated archway to the chancel is just a plain semi-circle of great blocks of chiselled granite. The windows are equally primitive in design – that window in the east end to catch the morning sun in the altar area, and those two tiny apertures in the south wall.

In striking contrast to Reefert Church stands the Priory of St Saviour, supposedly founded by Laurence O'Toole. It is set in a grove of fir trees about one mile east of the monastic city, and also consists of a nave and chancel church, but with an annexe on the north side thought to have been the living quarters of monks – or, more probably, nuns. Its outstanding features are the ornate Romanesque archway between the nave and chancel, and the equally ornate east window of the originally barrel-vaulted chancel.

Reefert Church Interior

Besides ordinary convents for nuns, double monasteries with a house for monks and one for nuns – that for nuns discreetly segregated at a distance from that for the men – were probably more prevalent from the very beginning of the early Irish monastic system than the paltry record shows. The classic instance was the fifth-century foundation of Kildare by Ireland's patroness, St Brigid. Founded for nuns, it soon had a separate residence for monks, the nuns being subject to an abbess and the monks to an abbot or bishop, with St Brigid – and later her successor abbesses – presiding over both houses. St Saviour's Priory at Glendalough, and the twelfth-century Nuns' Church at Clonmacnois to be mentioned shortly, are witness to the continuation of the practice of double houses. There were dissenting voices, of course; as late as 1228, the Visitor Stephen of Lexington was railing against the proximity of nunneries to the Cistercian monasteries at Mellifont and Jerpoint.

Location: Glendalough, 25m (40km) south of Dublin City. Visitor Centre open daily.

CLONMACNOIS
County Offaly

Glendalough is remembered as one of the few great monastic cities for which Ireland was once famous – another is Clonmacnois, which like Glendalough, began as a spiritual retreat for its founder, St Ciarán (kee-rawn), and his companions. But within seven months of its mid-sixth-century founding, Ciarán was dead – of the yellow plague, it was said. So the growth of Clonmacnois followed the death of its founder and its brilliance as a great collegiate school and centre of early Irish art, which attracted thousands of students and survived countless plunderings and burnings, continued over several centuries. By the time of its final devastation in 1552 by an English garrison from Athlone, the celebrated monastic settlement had long passed the peak of its fame. All that is now left is a group of ruined churches, two Round Towers, a couple of sculptured crosses, and many inscribed grave slabs. The time span of the making of all these is from about 800 to 1200.

Clonmacnois is situated on the east bank of the River Shannon at the geographical centre of Ireland, in a terrain that is flat and featureless; in this it is far removed from the sequestered beauty of Glendalough. But if viewed in a quiet hour – a rare event in season – it has its own special charm. Occupying as it did a border position between Connacht and what was then called Meath, and a strategic location at the junction of the Esker Riada and Shannon, it was inevitable that Clonmacnois should become something of a pawn in the struggle for supremacy between the Uí Néill Kings of Meath and the O'Connor Kings of Connaught. However, it did benefit by royal patronage and protection in return for prayers and burial rights.

Clonmacnois was not named a bishopric at the Synod of Rathbreasail in 1111 because of its resistance to new church reforms, but the clergy and chieftains of Meath quickly reversed that decision and it became the cathedral church of west Meath. By the mid-thirteenth century, however, the diocese of Clonmacnois had been reduced to only a small area east of the Shannon, Anglo-Norman ecclesiastical encroachment being accorded the blame.

Replicas of the Cross of the Scriptures and the nearby South Cross greet the visitor on entering the monastic enclosure: the originals have been moved inside the Visitor Centre for better preservation. The distinctive feature of the Irish High Cross is the ring encircling the cross at the junction of the shaft and crossarm, and the scriptural reference indicates that the carvings on the cross include scenes from the Old and New Testaments. Identifiable subjects are the Last Judgment and episodes from the Passion and Death of Christ. The dating of the Cross of the Scriptures to the early years of the tenth century gives it a direct relationship to the superlative Muiredach's Cross at Monasterboice, County Louth. The South Cross is not scriptural; it *has* a Crucifixion scene, but the emphasis is on elaborate ornamentation.

Temple Doolin is reputedly the earliest church at Clonmacnois. It certainly conforms well to the typical primitive Irish stone church with antae on the west gable, a round-headed window on the east side, and no windows on the north side, but the lintelled doorway formerly on the west side was replaced in 1689 by the present plain Gothic style doorway as part of a restoration carried out by one Edmund Dowling, from whom the tiny church gets its name. This restoration may account also for Temple Hurpan on the east side of Temple Doolin.

A short distance ahead is Temple Rí (Church of the King), or Temple Melaghlin, to name its founder. Melaghlin held sway over the local family of MacCoghlans, to whose territory the diocese of Clonmacnois had about shrunk in the Anglo-Norman advance. The narrow twin windows in the east wall of the Church are the main feature of interest. They are round-arched, widely splayed on the interior, and framed by a pointed roll moulding, and in anticipation of similar windows to be encountered at Clonfert and Ballintubber, they

Aerial View of Clonmacnois

exemplify a late Romanesque style that continued in many western establishments until the mid-thirteenth century. That so late a church of the size of Temple Rí should be built here is an index of the continued vitality of Clonmacnois at that time.

The Cathedral, which dates from 909, was built by Colman, Abbot of Clonmacnois and Clonard, under the patronage of the Uí Néill High King of Ireland, Flann Sinna. It was burned by the Vikings in 985. Restoration about 1100 just preceded the elevation of Clonmacnois to diocesan status. Further restoration was undertaken in 1336 courtesy of the King of Moylurg, Tomaltach MacDermot, and the Cathedral then became known as Temple Dermot. Architecturally speaking, the Cathedral's finest hour came in the mid-fifteenth century with the insertion of the magnificent north doorway by Dean Odo shortly before his death in 1461; it is of three orders with the jambs flowing up into the arches without the usual intervening capitals, and all the jambs and arches are moulded in a series of roll mouldings and hollows. The hood moulding over the outer arch has a vine scroll ornament on the face and a conventional crocketed leaf design around the crest. The pilasters that frame the doorway on each side have beautifully carved pinnacles, and a horizontal cornice across the top is inscribed with the names of the three carved figures below it – Saints Dominic, Patrick, and Francis. Of comparable quality and design is the 1471 west wall doorway of the Augustinian priory of Clontuskert, west of Clonmacnois.

The tiny dilapidated Temple Ciarán was built on or close to the site of St Ciarán's own earlier wooden oratory, and was revered as the tomb-shrine of the saint. In its proximity to the Cathedral it parallels the case of Glendalough, where the Priests' House is reputedly the tomb-shrine of St Kevin. On the northern edge of the monastic site there is a twelfth-century church and Round Tower combination – Temple Finghin (fih-neen') and McCarthy's Tower – which is alone of its kind in Ireland. The Finian of the name is uncertain: perhaps St Ciarán's tutor St Finian of Clonard? The church is

North Doorway of Cathedral

nave-and-chancel in type but the nave has virtually disappeared leaving the chancel arch with its Romanesque chevron ornamentation exposed. The Round Tower is only 56 feet (17 metres) in height, with a doorway at ground level facing north, and all windows facing south with none just below the cap. The question as to whether the Tower and church are contemporary has long been debated, but the weight of scholarly judgment leans to the conclusion that they are – that here is just a simple combination of church and belfry tower similar to St Kevin's Church at Glendalough.

O'Rourke's Tower has been credited to Fergal O'Rourke, King of Connaught, who died in 964: it was actually completed as late as 1124. Its present topless condition has been variously attributed to a dispute between monks and masons over building costs, a lightning storm of 1135 that demolished the upper part, and damage done when the bells were being removed in 1552 by those English soldiers from Athlone. It is a pity, as the quality of the stonework in the lower part is unmatched in Round Towers anywhere in Ireland – except, perhaps, at Ardmore, County Waterford – with the limestone worked in regular courses and the doorway surmounted by a round-headed regular arch of nine stones.

There is an extension to Clonmacnois in the form of the Nuns' Church situated a short distance to the east of the main group of ruins. It is known that nuns were established at Clonmacnois since the early years of the eleventh century, but what remains today of the Nuns' Church dates from about 1160 with restoration work dating from 1867. Little remains besides the Romanesque doorway and chancel arch. Tradition has it that these ornate pieces were provided by Dervorgilla, wife of Tiernan O'Rourke, King of Breffny (modern Counties Cavan and Leitrim). This naughty lady had an extra-marital liaison with Dermot MacMurrough, King of Leinster, which resulted in O'Rourke's attacking Leinster and MacMurrough's precipitating the Anglo-Norman invasion of Ireland as a reprisal. In a spirit of deep repentance, Dervorgilla retired to Clonmacnois for a time on the death of her husband in 1172, where she generously endowed the nunnery.

Nun's Church, Clonmacnois

In a quiet water'd land, a land of roses
Stands Saint Kieran's city fair;
And the warriors of Erin in their famous generations
Slumber there.

Rolleston's poem makes romantic mention of the names of many that lie beneath the hallowed earth of Clonmacnois. The modern day traveller cannot commune with these, but can at least inspect some of the memorial or grave slabs for which Clonmacnois is famous. A Greek or Latin form cross usually dominates the design, and the plea 'Ór do' (ore duh) followed by the name of the person commemorated, asks for a prayer for the deceased. Of such is the real legacy of Clonmacnois.

Location: 13m (21km) south of Athlone. Visitor Centre open daily.

GALLARUS ORATORY
Dingle Peninsula, County Kerry

Use of stone is one stage in the search for imperishable building materials. Before the introduction of lime mortar for binding purposes, the circular corbelled drystone clochán represented an early product of that search. The corbelling method is at least as old as the roofs of chambers of Neolithic passage graves, like Newgrange in County Meath, built on this principle. The corbel vault suited the round plan ideally because the circular ring created at each course countered any tendency of the wall to inward collapse. But alas! applied to larger structures built on a rectangular plan, the corbelling technique tended to fail, as witness the many early stone oratories that have collapsed.

Gallarus Oratory, however, is different. It is a rectangular corbelled vault unique in Ireland in being the only example among some twenty of its kind remaining in almost perfect condition. Its position is at the west end of the Dingle Peninsula, the most northerly of the long peninsulas of Kerry, a wild mountainous region of great natural beauty. The model for Gallarus may well be found in the *bori* of Provence, which were rectangular huts of corbelled flagstones with straight ridged roofs. It is known that after the beginning of Christianity in Ireland missionaries plied back and forth to the Continent in a two-way dissemination of knowledge.

Gallarus was formerly a landmark close to the old Saint's Road that ran northwards via Kilmalkedar Church to the summit of Mount Brandon. A centuries-old annual pilgrimage to the summit passed along this path on the feast day of St Brendan, from whom the mountain may get its name. The name of Gallarus itself remains an enigma – the House of the Foreigners. What foreigners? No one seems to know.

Equally open to question is the date of its construction. Its drystone composition argues for an early construction, but its very perfection persuades the judgment to put it later in the scale of building. The earliest reasonable dating would probably be eighth century. As early as the seventh century the Irish missionaries on the Continent must have come in contact with the use of mortar in building, so that its introduction into Ireland cannot have come too much later than that. One can reasonably assume that use of mortared stone would then have become the prevailing choice.

The exterior of Gallarus Oratory resembles a well-made stack of turf. All four walls curve inwards from the ground up, with the end gables having less inward inclination than the sides; taken with the thickness of the walls, this contributes to the stability of the structure. The west door has a flat stone lintel and a batter or inward sloping of the jambs, both characteristic features of early Irish church building. The interior is a dark but not a damp one, due to the slight downward inclination of the bed-joints of the stonework that directs the rain away from the building.

Gallarus Oratory

In spite of the near-perfection of Gallarus, the side walls do sag inwards a little halfway between ground and roof ridge. Only the exceptional selection and shaping of the stones, and the meticulous craftsmanship expended upon them, have postponed for Gallarus the fate of all other similar structures.

Among the poems of Ireland's foremost living poet and Nobel Prize recipient, Séamus Heaney, is one entitled *In Gallarus Oratory*. Standing alongside the Oratory, with Mount Brandon in the distance and Smerwick Harbour in the foreground, the visitor might try to capture the essence of the poet's lines:

> You can still feel the community pack
> This place: its like going into a turfstack,
> A core of old dark walled up with stone
> A yard thick. When you're in it alone
> You might have dropped, a reduced creature
> To the heart of the globe ...

Location: 2m (4km) east of Ballyferriter beside the R559. Direct access year-round.

CORMAC'S CHAPEL
Rock of Cashel, County Tipperary

As far back as the fourth century there was a concentration of power in the hands of a dynasty whose leaders were the acknowledged kings of Munster, with Cashel as their capital, and the celebrated Rock of Cashel remained chief residence of these Munster kings until 1101. In that year, as recorded in the *Annals of the Four Masters*, King Murtagh O'Brien 'granted Cashel of the Kings to the religious, without any claim of layman or cleric upon it, but to the religious of Ireland in general.'A decade later Cashel was selected as the second archbishopric of Ireland, complementing that of Armagh in the north.

Ireland's first and finest Romanesque church known as Cormac's Chapel was erected between 1127 and 1134 by the king-bishop of Cashel, Cormac MacCarthy. Built of sandstone ashlar, and protected by its unique stone roof, it remains well preserved, but there is a tough ongoing fight against dampness. Due to potent English and Continental influences it broke almost completely with Irish building styles; because of this and the unusually ambitious scope of its architectural and decorative details, it had a minimal effect on Irish church building elsewhere.

Cormac's Chapel is of the nave-and-chancel type. Prominent imported features are the exterior blind wall arcading and the tall square towers set on opposite sides of the east end of the nave. Appearing almost as transepts, these towers add a special measure of grandeur to the Chapel. Oddly enough, they are not quite matching; the tower on the south side is smaller and flat-topped, while the northern one has a roof of pyramidal shape. Both towers, however, are attractively banded with string-courses (eight on the south tower) at the levels of the different storeys. A spiral stairway leads to the south tower belfry, and an ornamental doorway leading from the north tower into the nave suggests perhaps a ceremonial internal entrance.

The approach is from the south side where the four-storey wall exterior has three levels of blind arcading, the third level with eight semi-circular arches being the most impressive. Rectangular windows later inserted to light the interior destroy the second level.

The main doorway was originally on the north side to face the Round Tower. When the adjacent thirteenth-century Cathedral was built it hemmed in the north doorway on that side. Because this remarkable doorway of six orders is among the most impressive products of Irish Romanesque art, one is baffled by the unenlightened decisions made here. The doorway jambs are crowned by capitals which are scalloped, or carved with human masks and grotesque animals. Chevrons adorn the arches and the tympanum is carved with a large beast, probably a lion, crushing its prey while being attacked by a centaur wearing headgear and armed with bow and arrow. Over the doorway is a steep pediment decorated with running chevrons and rosettes.

The barrel-vaulted ceiling of the nave is reinforced by five thick unmoulded arch ribs that spring from short rounded engaged columns with mainly scalloped capitals. These semi-circular transverse rings – already found in larger Continental Romanesque churches – made it possible to achieve a reduction in the thickness of the vault shell, and to construct the ceiling as a set of separate bays. The engaged columns rest on a broad shelf along the side walls of the nave. Below this shelf semi-circular arches form a chevron-decorated blank arcade carried on flat pilasters ornamented with geometrical designs.

Lavish ornamentation was the norm, and it extended to the chancel, entered through a high arch of four orders. Roll mouldings and chevrons adorn the orders, but of greatest interest are the human heads carved along the second order. Rows of heads are a recurring theme among the Romanesque carvers – at Clonfert and Inchagoill, County Galway, and at Dysert O'Dea, County Clare, for example. Are they representations of saints or notable personages? a Christianisation of the pagan Celtic head cult? or just ornamentation?

Cormac's Chapel

The side walls of the chancel are arcaded in a manner somewhat similar to those of the nave, and the ceiling has heavy rounded groin ribs that spring from engaged columns at the corners of the room – perhaps the first such vaulted ceiling in Ireland.

Surveying the dank interior of Cormac's Chapel today, it is hard to picture the day when it was bathed in rich warm colours, but a small window into the past has recently been opened by a partial restoration of the colourful ceiling frescoes in the chancel area.

Sarcophagus, Cormac's Chapel

Against the west wall of the nave is a large carved stone sarcophagus with an elaborate eleventh-century ribbon-beast interlacement carving on its front face. Two quadrupeds with ribbon-like bodies intertwined form the theme, and the style is called Urnes from a wooden church in Norway that featured elaborate carvings in this style. Considering Ireland's long contact with the Vikings, it is not surprising that Scandinavian influences should finally penetrate Irish art work. It is of interest to observe here that the panel of interlaced beasts on the base of St Patrick's Cross (now preserved in the nearby Hall of the Vicars Choral) is of similar

44

style and vintage. The missing covering slab of the sarcophagus was reputedly ornamented with a cross and the name Cormac, giving rise to the belief that here indeed was the tomb of Cormac McCarthy, the builder of this remarkable Chapel.

Location: Rock of Cashel, Cashel. Visitor Centre open daily.

KILMALKEDAR CHURCH
Dingle Peninsula, County Kerry

Whatever direction the course of European Christianity was taking in the twelfth century, it could not have pushed further west than the outpost of Kilmalkedar, overlooking historic Smerwick Harbour at the western extremity of the Dingle Peninsula. St Malkedar was long dead when the twelfth-century Kilmalkedar Church was founded. His death had been recorded in the *Martyrology of Donegal*: 'AD636 – Maolcethair, Son of the King of Uladh of Cill Melchedair, near the shore of the sea to the west of Brandon Hill.' However much the local cult of the Saint has since been displaced in favour of Brendan the Navigator, Malkedar is remembered in the little church of his name.

On the Dingle Peninsula the pagan god Crom Dubh was believed to have inhabited an area close to Mount Brandon. The annual Christianised festival of Lughnasa (loo'-nasa) that took place on Crom Dubh Sunday was a celebration of Christian victory over Crom Dubh. It took the form of a pilgrimage to Mount Brandon, Kilmalkedar being the most important station on the route, and the main symbol of the suppression of pagan worship in the territory of the Corca Dhuibhne (kurka gweeneh) people.

Apart from its association with the triumph of Christianity, Kilmalkedar Church is significant as the only Irish Romanesque church on the peninsula. In many details it so agrees with Cormac's Chapel on the Rock of Cashel that the influence of the latter on its construction cannot be doubted – it is known, for instance, that the Corca Dhuibhne people actually lived in subjection to their Gaelic overlords in Cashel. As at Cashel there are wall arcades on both sides of the Kilmalkedar nave – five half-round columns, with blank arcading in the spaces between them, set along a horizontal shelf well above ground level, with scalloped capitals merging into the only surviving lower courses of the corbelled roof. The tympanum in the badly scarred west doorway is another feature that Kilmalkedar shares with Cormac's Chapel.

Kilmalkedar Church

Approaching from the west side up a moderate hillside slope, one is struck by the warm blend of colours in the local sandstone of the steeply pitched west gable. Striking also is the strong batter, that inward sloping of walls, doorways, and windows commonly found in early Irish church buildings; architecturally it served the practical purpose of stability, but its usefulness as an aesthetic refinement cannot have gone unnoticed. In imitation of the elbow-cruck structure of earlier timber buildings, antae protrude from each side of the gable wall, tapering towards the roof ridge and ending in winged finials.

The nave of Kilmalkedar dates from about 1150 and the chancel is a little later. Both appear to have had corbelled stone roofs of triangular shape and straight-sided form. The ultimate instance of this kind of roof, which has been restored, is that of the tiny MacDara's Church on the island of that name off the coast of Galway. With the aid of inside timber cross-props such roofs could have been given an extended lease of life, provided the pitch was steep, the span short, and the general construction sufficiently massive – and the chancel in Kilmalkedar would have qualified in all these areas. But like most churches that used the corbelling technique the entire roof of Kilmalkedar has collapsed.

Several typically Romanesque art motifs are employed in the two-order deeply-cut chancel arch: on the outer arch a roll moulding bordered by a row of disks; on the inner arch chevrons along the sides, lozenges filled with floral patterns on the soffit, the different components accentuated by fillets of V-section; supporting jambs with engaged colonettes topped by scalloped capitals. Almost identical patterns are found at Annaghdown in County Galway, Cashel in County Tipperary, Glendalough in County Wicklow, and elsewhere.

Among the many gravestones in the cemetery facing the Church are two carved stones of special interest. The first is a holed Ogham stone, easily identified from the series of parallel notches cut along its edge. Ogham is the earliest Irish writing and was in use from about AD300 to 800, or later. In the Ogham alphabet letters consist of number, length,

Chancel Arch, Kilmalkedar Church

inclination, and position of strokes. Inscriptions in Ogham are of the short commemorative type. Holed stones are probably pre-Christian in origin, and their purpose is not known. The second is a sundial. It is carved on one face, which is roughly semi-circular, with three radii that may have marked the hours of terce (9am), sext (12pm), and none (3pm), times usually associated with canonical offices in a monastic context – or in the case of Kilmalkedar with perhaps the times of special prayer on days of pilgrimage. The hole at the centre was for the metal gnomon, now long gone, which threw the shadow line across the sundial face, indicating the time, and the religious association is reinforced by the stylised cross of arcs carved on the other face of the stone.

Location: About 4m (6.5km) north of Milltown. Direct access.

ST LASERIAN'S CATHEDRAL
Old Leighlin, County Carlow

A seventh-century monastery was founded at Old Leighlin – then called Leighlin (lock-lin) – by St Gobban, whose successor Laserian (+639) was ordained a priest by Pope Gregory the Great and possibly consecrated bishop by Pope Honorius I. Laserian's fame was as abbot of a flourishing monastic establishment said to have housed at one time an incredible 1,500 monks. His cult was later boosted by a legend that, to expiate for his sins, he willingly endured illness caused by thirty diseases at once.

Leighlin was confirmed as one of the five dioceses of Leinster in 1152. The Irish Church was now reorganised in firm subjection to Rome: this, combined with the recent arrival of the Cistercians, signalled the end of the old Irish monastic way of life. So the beginnings of St Laserian's under Donatus, bishop of Leighlin (1152-81), occurred at a most significant moment in Irish church history. By the century's end, the election of Anglo-Norman bishops to Leighlin initiated a period of strife that lasted 200 years. Before the return of Irish bishops in the fifteenth century Leighlin had frequently been plundered by the 'wild Irish', and at one point the bishop and chapter had even requested that the see be moved to a more peaceable place.

At its completion about the end of the thirteenth century, the Cathedral consisted of a very long chancel and slightly wider aisleless nave, to which north and south transepts were soon added. The north transept is now roofless, and the south transept, where the side entrance to the church is located, no longer exists. The tower was inserted in the fifteenth century, and sixteenth century dates are given for the chapter house and for some reconstruction of the north and south chancel walls – work attributed to Bishop Matthew Sanders (1527-49), whose tomb is close to the sanctuary. Bishop Sanders' unfortunate predecessor was murdered by his archdeacon with whom he had quarrelled. The grave of the murdered Bishop Maurice Doran is marked by a floor slab in the chancel.

The chapter house – originally the Lady Chapel, a medieval expression of the cult of the Virgin Mary – which was added to the north side of the chancel, fell into ruin and was re-roofed about 1865 at the expense of the Archdeacon of Leighlin. As the medieval period advanced, every church of consequence had a Lady Chapel, a religious model in the quest for the perfect woman of knightly chivalry. From 1899 is dated the wooden ceiling of the chancel. In 1926 the chancel walls were stripped of their rough plaster facing to expose the underlying light grey stone that now gives them their rich natural beauty. The quality of the masonry in the four-light east window of the chancel has received reserved comment. It dates from the second quarter of the sixteenth century. The main fault in the design lies in the fact that the switchlines in the upper half of the window are parallel instead of converging, but the stained glass insertions add rich warm colour to the chancel. They are in memory of Mary Louise Helen Vigors who died in 1933. The three-light east window of the adjacent chapter house with its hint of flamboyant tracery has a more attractive design. In sad contrast to the richness of the chancel stand the flat whitewashed walls of the nave, with no windows in the north and south walls, light entering only from four skylights in the roof and a clear-glass three-light window in the west wall. The contrast between the humble nave with its strange lighting system and the proud chancel with its stained glass is further emphasised by the panelled glass screen with retractable doors that now separates them; it was inserted in 1955, when the nave was no longer needed for regular church services.

There is a simple dignity about the sanctuary area with its curtained reredos. Four steps of black Kilkenny marble leading up to the altar were laid in 1916, when the floor was also laid with grey Cork marble. A four-seat stone sedilia with attractive trefoil arches is set below the two large windows in the south wall, and is unique in Ireland in having one seat more than the usual three. The pulpit is a sad memorial to the Dean of Leighlin, John Finlay, who was murdered in 1921 in connection with the Troubles.

The oldest furnishing in St Laserian's is the black marble eleventh-century baptismal font in the chancel under the tower area; the more decorated font standing by the south door of the nave dates from 1225, and was brought here from St Mary's Church in Gowran, County Kilkenny. High on the list of significant furnishings in any Christian church has always been the baptismal font. Ancient fonts were prominently mounted stone structures, their sides frequently carved with baptismal and other designs, their tops fitted with wooden covers of sometimes elaborate design and large enough to permit of the complete immersion of infants. Old medieval fonts are a rarity in Irish churches, so that when they do occur they are indeed treasures to be observed and valued.

The ribbed vault under the tower is a scaled-down copy of that erected by Bishop Hackett (1460-78) over the crossing of St Canice's Cathedral in the next-door diocese of Kilkenny. There are seven main ribs with subsidiary lierne ribs forming a pattern around the centre of the vault.

Most of the memorials are to members of the Vigors family – the stained glass in the chancel has already been mentioned. The Vigors are the descendants of Bartholomew Vigors, Bishop of Ferns and Leighlin, who died in 1722. The earliest memorial is to Urban Vigors, who was High Sheriff of County Carlow and died in 1718. Cathedral restorations of the nineteenth century owed much to the interest and benefactions of the Vigors.

St Laserian's is an historic building of great charm that continues to exude a strong medieval atmosphere, and is among the privileged handful of smaller early cathedrals that are *not* in ruins. Another is Killaloe Cathedral in County Clare, which also retains much of its thirteenth-century appearance and atmosphere, and more than a passing interior resemblance to St Laserian's.

Location: About 9m (14.5km) south of Carlow and about 2m (3km) west of the N9.

JERPOINT ABBEY
Thomastown, County Kilkenny

The Cistercians were brought to Ireland in 1142 and founded their first monastery at Mellifont in County Louth. By about 1200, they had 25 abbeys, five of Anglo-Norman origin. When the Anglo-Normans attempted to gain control of Irish abbeys in districts they had recently grasped from the Irish, the seeds of a long conflict were planted. Irish monks also opposed the full Cistercian observance and their forced subservience to a French General Chapter. Visitors appointed to inspect and reform were sometimes refused entry, physical resistance being mounted by armed monks and lay brothers.

The early years of Jerpoint were enlivened by this kind of dissension. This Abbey may have been founded about 1160 for the Benedictines by Donal MacGillapatrick, king of Ossory, and then taken over in 1180 as a daughter-house of the Cistercian abbey of Baltinglass in County Wicklow. The Benedictine connection is an arguable one, but there is evidence that it provided a convenient interim classification for some early communities of Irish monks waiting for Cistercian affiliation. Whatever the origin, the monks of Jerpoint robustly supported their Irish confrères elsewhere in a unified resistance to French reforms. In 1227 the abbot of Jerpoint was deposed for instigating, during an official Visitation, what was called the Riot of Jerpoint, and the Abbey was then placed under the watchful eye of Fountains in England. A standing dispute, not resolved until 1362 when Jerpoint relinquished all claims to it, was the transfer of Killenny, a daughter-house of Jerpoint, to the rival Anglo-Norman Duiske Abbey in nearby Graignamanagh. During the fifteenth century Jerpoint appears to have enjoyed a certain prosperity under the patronage of the Butler Earls of Ormond. It was dissolved by Henry VIII in 1540. The abbot and five remaining monks left, and the Abbey possessions were leased to James, 9th Earl of Ormond.

North Arcade of Nave

The architectural challenge facing the early abbey builders was that of providing a monastic layout for a self-supporting community of men isolated from the world. The

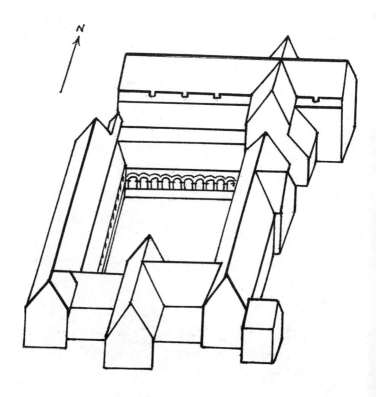

Cistercian Abbey Elevation

Cistercians found the solution in an abbey plan seen in various stages of survival across the Irish landscape – a plan so standard, it was said, that if a blind monk were moved from one monastery to another he would immediately know his way around. The plan divided the abbey complex into four ranges built around an open cloister garth surrounded by a covered walkway giving access to all the cloistral buildings. In the north range was the cruciform church. The east range served the needs of the choir monks and consisted of sacristy, chapter house, parlour, slype, and dayroom on the

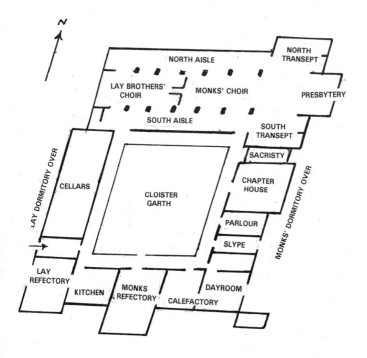

N

Cistercian Abbey Plan

ground floor and dormitory overhead. The west range
contained the cellars of the house and lay brothers' refectory,
with lay dormitory overhead. The south range had the
monks' refectory in the centre, the kitchen at the west end,
and the calefactory or warming room on the east side. In an
open space to the east stood the abbot's house, infirmary, and
monks' burial ground.

The daily routine of the Cistercian choir monks centred
around church offices, chanted seven times daily,
commencing with Vigils at 2.00 am. It also included manual

labour and study. Lay brothers looked after the practical monastic chores, and the management of the abbey granges.

Architecturally, Jerpoint is an amalgam of three successive styles: Romanesque, Transitional, and Gothic. The bulk of it is Romanesque or Transitional (1160-1200), but the tower and cloister arcade date from after 1400.

The ruins of Jerpoint have an attraction beyond those of any other Cistercian abbey in Ireland. Church and transepts are largely intact except for the south arcade and wall of the nave, as is the ground floor of the east range. Only fragments of the south range remain, and nothing at all of the west range. Parts of the cloister arcade were reconstructed in 1953.

Immediately ahead of the visitor entrance are the bluntly-pointed arches of the north arcade of the nave begun about 1170. These are supported on short robust piers varying in shape from cylindrical to square, to octagonal with engaged corner shafts, built over the rough-looking perpyn walls that were originally hidden by the stepped wooden stalls of the monks placed along the arcade on both sides. Capitals under square abaci are mainly scalloped, but at the east end there is some beaded strapwork and floral patterning over a scalloped base, and beaded zigzags combined with floral designs. In a feature peculiar to most Irish Cistercian houses the clerestory windows are placed over the piers, not the arches. Those L-shaped foundation walls across the nave halfway along its length mark the dividing line between the monks' choir, which extended to the presbytery (chancel) on the east, and that of the lay brothers on the west. The three round-headed west windows of the nave are Romanesque with ashlar masonry framing widely-splayed interiors.

The east end presbytery and transepts are the earliest parts of Jerpoint. Jambs and string courses of three earlier Romanesque windows are still visible on the exterior of the short presbytery, but the existing traceried window is fourteenth century. In the north transept the character of Irish Romanesque is apparent in the small round-headed windows with inclined jambs and in the Irish-style side chapel capitals. Burgundian influence appears in the pointed arches of the

Jerpoint Abbey Tower

transept chapels and presbytery, and the barrel vaults all along the east range. The Cistercians chose barrel-vaulting as a cheap and structurally sound way of roofing small spaces. Timber side-screens originally continued the monks' choir right past the nave arcades as far as the presbytery step beyond which stood the high altar. The transepts were thus cut off from the monks' choir and were reached from the choir by door openings in the side-screens. In this way the church offices were conducted in a completely enclosed space, directed towards the high altar. Carvings by the famous fifteenth-sixteenth century O'Tunney stone sculptors of Callan, County Kilkenny, are found on the medieval tombs in the side chapels of the north transept, with characteristically stylised treatment of hairdressing and draperies in the squat figures of the apostles. The inscription *Roricus OTuyne scripsit* identifies the work of the best known of these Ossory masters as found at Jerpoint, Kilcooly (County Tipperary), and in St Canice's Cathedral, Kilkenny.

Rib-vaulting occurs only in the crossing under the tower, but along with the tower itself, the tallest and finest of Cistercian towers, this is fifteenth-century work. In the south transept the wooden steps, which now replace the original night stairs, lead up to an open flagged space formerly occupied by the monks' dormitory. Summoned by the bell at two o'clock in the morning, each monk would leave his mattress, and shuffle down the night stairs to the church for the office of Vigils.

Cistercian cloister arcades were always attached to the cloistral buildings by lean-to roofs, and from the evidence of the remnants that have survived, they do show some stylistic development. The earliest and typical arcades, found at Mellifont, show semi-circular arches carried on paired colonettes; by about 1300 arches might be trefoiled, as at Baltinglass, County Wicklow; later again arches might be traceried, as at Holy Cross, County Tipperary. Surprising then that the Jerpoint cloister arcade of the 1400s reverts to simple semi-circular chamfered arches carried on supports of the dumbbell type; that is, paired colonettes cut out of one block of stone and linked together by narrow panels. These panels, and frequently the capitals and bases, provide the canvasses

Crossing and North Transept

for a fascinating display of sculptured figures and animals –
saints, ecclesiastics, knights, noble ladies, and grotesque
beasts. The significance of all the cloister carvings cannot be

Cloister Sculpture at Jerpoint

deciphered but the following are among those that are identifiable:

An abbot with cowl, staff, large rosary beads, and right hand raised in blessing;

A bishop with crozier and fingers raised in blessing;

An aristocratic lady with long pleated dress, her hands inside fitchets (slits), with lappets (streamers) at the elbow extending to the bottom of the dress;

The fourth-century Catherine of Alexandria with sword and broken wheel, the instruments of her martyrdom;

St Margaret of Antioch, patroness of childbirth, beheaded in the persecution of the Roman Emperor, Diocletian (245-313);

An Ormond knight with shield;

A comical figure reminiscent of a court jester;

A dragon with long twisting tail.

The exuberant sculpture is altogether at odds with Cistercian austerity, and, because of loss and arbitrary reconstruction, its theme (if it ever had any) must remain a mystery.

Location: 1m (2.5km) south-west of Thomastown. Visitor Centre open mid-April to mid-October.

BOYLE ABBEY
Boyle, County Roscommon

Boyle Abbey forms an early strand in the web of Cistercian expansion in Ireland. It was colonised from Mellifont in 1161 and patronised by the MacDermots, Irish Lords of Moylurg in the northern part of the county. Friction between Irish and French factions destructive of the peace of such Irish houses as Mellifont and Jerpoint extended also to Boyle, resulting in attacks on the Abbey by the Anglo-Norman William de Burgo in 1202, delays in the completion of the nave, and forced transfer of the allegiance of Boyle from Mellifont to the French mother-house of Clairvaux. Boyle appears to have survived the suppression of the monasteries under Henry VIII, partly because of its western position, and partly because it was only a monastery in name by that time. It lost some of its monastic appearance when it became a military establishment called Boyle Castle in the period from about 1600 to 1800.

Most of what is left of Boyle Abbey is the church – presbytery, transepts, tower, north and south arcades of the nave, and west gable. The outer walls of the church, along with the cloisters and domestic buildings, no longer exist. Fortunately, the surviving parts of the church are in a remarkably good state of preservation, making Boyle Abbey well worth a visit. A study of the Transitional features combining Romanesque and Early Gothic architectural styles is one of two main ingredients in the enjoyment of Boyle Abbey; the other is the artistic carving on the many capitals.

The presbytery and transepts are the earliest parts, begun about 1165, a date approximately matching that of the east end at Jerpoint, so that the similarity to Jerpoint is quite remarkable, with Burgundian influences in the pointed arches and barrel vaults of the presbytery and transept chapels. Initially, the presbytery had Romanesque round-headed windows with string courses extending across the east wall. In a move towards Gothic, these windows were replaced during the early 1200s by the existing three tall lancets.

The tower is located at the intersection of the presbytery, nave, and transepts – that is, over the crossing. Typically, Cistercian towers were later additions. By about 1450 crossing towers were regarded as an essential adjunct to the church. Depending on local emphasis, a tower might act as a belfry; it might provide additional accommodation, possibly for the abbot; equipped with battlements, it might have a defensive function, however poorly placed for defence. And it had potential as a prestige symbol. Opinions differ as to whether the Boyle tower was part of the original building. In this regard, the fact that the western arch of the crossing, which rests on corbels with thirteenth-century Early English nailhead ornaments, is different from the other three, indicates that the tower was a later addition to the building.

View the nave in the dual role of architect and art lover. Just the north and south arcades remain, each with eight bays in recognisably good condition. English influence, as distinct from Burgundian, now makes its appearance, and inspection of the arcades reveals three different building phases over the period c.1175-1220, with a possible pause between the second

Aerial View of Boyle Abbey

South Arcade of Nave

and third due to the sacking of the Abbey in 1202. The first four bays of the south arcade at the east end belong to the earliest phase. Round arches of two orders are supported by substantial cylindrical piers with scalloped capitals and octagonal abaci, and bases are square with foliage spurs at the corners. To the second phase, continuing until about 1200, belong the corresponding four bays of the north arcade: there is a startling change to pointed arches of two orders supported by piers consisting of a cluster of eight shafts, the central shaft of each cluster cutting upwards through the abacus to form a wall corbel. Vertical wooden posts resting on these wall corbels supported the framework of the wooden roof of the nave. To the third phase, ending about 1220, belong the remaining west side arches of both the north and south arcades. Arches were continued round-headed on the south side and pointed on the north, but piers were changed from cylindrical to square, chamfered at the angles, and with triple shafts on the inner faces to support the inner order of the arch, and relieve the prosaic squareness of the piers.

In the role of art lover the observer can now turn to the artistic carvings on the many capitals throughout the church. Spartan Cistercian attitudes looked askance at ornamentation as unbecoming a monastic environment, but Boyle somehow managed to be an exception: reasons include the Irish monks' resistance to the rigours of the Rule as interpreted by their French brethren, and the lateness of Boyle, which exposed it to the lure of Irish monasteries elsewhere, in particular the contemporary Augustinian Abbey of Ballintubber, County Mayo, which provided both the models and the masons for some of the work at Boyle.

In the presbytery, transepts, and north arcade of the nave, capital carvings show mainly foliage designs. Towards the east end of the south arcade the scalloped capital predominates, a borrowing from English Romanesque, with the scallop featured alone or as a base for stylised foliage

Capital Carving at Boyle

embellishment. But the prize pieces are found towards the west end of the south arcade, where the carvings are placed around the capitals without any break, like a frieze. Masterfully executed in high relief, the themes have no obvious religious meaning – a circle of little men with arms raised standing between trees, two dogs battling with cockerels over prey, two men in combat with lions, and a row of birds with long necks intertwined.

Location: Boyle

CLONFERT CATHEDRAL
Clonfert, County Galway

St Brendan the Navigator was one of Ireland's more dynamic saints. He lived from about 476 to about 575, and was active right along the west of Ireland, with monasteries to his name in Galway, Clare, and Kerry. And there is a suspicion that he beat Columbus by a thousand years to an epic crossing of the Atlantic Ocean in search of an island of promise. His monastery at Clonfert, on the west bank of the Shannon, a short distance to the north of Banagher, was one of two he founded in County Galway. That was in 563 and it survived in sufficient vigour after the Saint's death to be able to withstand the ten plunderings by the Vikings recorded in the *Annals of Clonmacnois*. Only the memory of those things remained when Clonfert was chosen as the centre of a diocese at the Synod of Rathbreasail in 1111. In 1152 a full national synod was held in Kells 'in order to set forth the Catholic Faith, to purify and correct the morals of the people, to consecrate four archbishops and give the pallia'. Its aim was reform, rooting out alleged flaws in the Irish system – lay hereditary abbacies, married clergy, bishops subject to abbots, lack of a parochial system and a general independence from Rome of the Irish Church. The work begun at Rathbreasail in 1111 was completed at Kells when the Papal Legate, Cardinal Paparo, brought the pallia for the four archbishops, adding Dublin and Tuam to Armagh and Cashel. At this Synod Clonfert was included as one of the suffragan churches of the new Archbishopric of Tuam, thus paving the way for Clonfert Cathedral, which was built in 1167 by the Irish chieftain Conor O'Kelly, Lord of Uí Máine (ee moyneh), of whose territory Clonfert was a part.

The building is not particularly large and was originally of the cruciform type, with north and south transepts and a fifteenth-century tower over the west end. However, the north transept has been removed and the south transept is in ruins. The Romanesque west doorway is the earliest feature of interest and is the crowning masterwork of its kind. No other existing Irish edifice can boast of an entrance of such distinction. The jambs consist of two broad outer pilasters and five orders of cylindrical engaged columns; a sixth order of blue limestone with carvings of two bishops and floral decoration is a fifteenth-century replacement. Each of the two outer pilasters and five engaged columns supports a semi-circular arch, making seven arches in red sandstone, along with the limestone arch that frames the door itself. Surmounting the arches is a tall pediment, framed by a double cable moulding and flanked at the pinnacle by two human masks. Its top part is made into a diaper of fifteen triangular panels, and ten inverted panels containing human heads; below this is an arcade with five round arches resting on six short pillars, and a human head peering out under each arch; two other heads are in the nooks between the end arches and the cable mouldings, with six further heads in the spandrels about the outer arch – a total of 25 human heads over the whole pediment. Each abacus has an upper fascia decorated with a running foliage scroll; below this a row of animal heads showing many expressions (more than 50 in a row right around the doorway). The capitals show a varied assortment of animals – two dragon heads, two cat-like masks, and three horse heads. Each pilaster and column supporting the arches is completely covered with its own particular pattern of decoration, and the designs include interlacings, chevrons extending into palmettes, zigzags, fret designs, along with geometrical and stylised foliage patterns. Each arch ring also features its own unique repeat design carved in very high relief – including a row of animal heads biting a roll.

The great west doorway will tend to monopolise the attention of the visitor, but among other features of special interest are the two limestone windows of the chancel, which, by contrast with the doorway, are virtually devoid of ornament. They date from the first half of the thirteenth century, up to a century after the west doorway. Late as they are, they remain thoroughly Romanesque in character.

Clonfert Cathedral

Viewed from the interior, the two windows are framed by bold roll mouldings. These in turn are enclosed by larger circular shafts which support the semi-circular hood mouldings. The central capital is carved with stiff-leaf foliage design, and those on the side are scalloped. Each light is flanked by four blank arcades also framed by roll mouldings. The balance and symmetry are altogether appealing but the unique feature in these windows is the close jointing of the large stones which gives the whole structure an almost seamless appearance, and places these windows among the finest of the late Romanesque group. Writing on ecclesiastical architecture in the nineteenth century, Richard Brash described the design as exceedingly chaste and beautiful, the mouldings simple and effective, and the workmanship superior to anything he had seen of either ancient or modern times.

About 30 miles (50km) from Clonfert on the Galway-Clare border is Kilmacduagh, the site of Ireland's famous leaning Round Tower and the ruins of a group of medieval churches, including one built for the Augustinian Canons by the Irish chieftain, Owen O'Heyne (+1253). The late Romanesque east windows of O'Heyne's Church are almost a match both in style and perfection of those at Clonfert, and argue for the same masons. Clonfert again made contact with Kilmacduagh when the two dioceses were united in 1602, a prologue to its present status as part of a union of all of eight former dioceses.

Clonfert Cathedral has received much interior remodelling, but the south jamb of the fifteenth-century chancel arch still exhibits a number of curious decorative carvings which appear to have been randomly placed. Some are carved in high relief and others are set into niches. Included are bunches of vine leaves and grapes, some angels under canopies, and a mermaid with comb and mirror. This last subject was a popular one in Gothic art, a sea image depicting the lure of sin.

With its modest appearance and seating for hardly more than 100 persons, Clonfert Cathedral is typical of many of the medieval cathedrals of Ireland – small buildings qualifying as cathedrals only because they house a bishop's chair and stalls for canons. Poverty, remoteness, political unrest, and religious

West Romanesque Doorway

dissension are among the factors of Irish life by which these churches have been shaped, the factors by which they must be judged to be understood.

Location: 8m (13km) southeast of Ballinasloe.

ST MARY'S CATHEDRAL
Limerick, County Limerick

From the early tenth century Limerick was a Viking
settlement. When Viking supremacy was terminated by the
Dalcassian King Brian Ború in 1014, Limerick became a key
Dalcassian stronghold, and when its first bishop, Gilbert,
presided as papal legate over the Synod of Rathbreasail in
1111, it was a foregone conclusion that Limerick would be
chosen as an episcopal see. Fifty years later its now ancient
cathedral was on the way to becoming a reality. As a place of
continued Christian worship St Mary's Cathedral is one of the
oldest in Ireland, and, among the medieval monuments of
historic Limerick, enjoys pride of place. It was founded about
1168 on the site of his former castle by that great builder of
churches Donal Mór O'Brien, King of Thomond. Donal Mór
was a major figure in the O'Brien dynasty of Munster when its
power was being challenged in the early years of the Anglo-
Norman invasion. He submitted to Henry II in 1171, thus
managing to retain much of his control of Clare and Limerick
during his lifetime.

The cruciform shape of the church, which followed the
Cistercian form, was completely altered by several fifteenth-
century side chapels added to the north and south aisles of
the nave. What remains of the late twelfth-century building is
the nave, its Transitional architectural style blending
Romanesque and Early Gothic features. Romanesque features
are the round-headed windows along the wall walks over the
side aisles, and the restored west door that must be viewed
from outside. Unfortunately, only the scalloped capitals on
opposite sides of the aisle walls give evidence of what was the
most interesting Romanesque feature, the former arches
across the aisles from north to south; these were of
Burgundian origin and unique in Ireland. Gothic features
appear in the four bluntly pointed arches of the nave, which
spring from robust square piers. Severity and simplicity are

the hallmarks of this style, infused as it is with the Cistercian spirit.

The present chancel dates from the fifteenth century. It has received several interim alterations, a notable one following its near destruction by cannon fire during the Williamite Siege of Limerick in 1691. A considerable amount of structural renovation was done during the nineteenth century. This included the installation of the east window of the chancel in 1860, and restoration of the south transept with the rebuilding of its five-light window in 1862. Except for the Caen stone pulpit erected after 1860, most of the chancel furnishings belong to this century. The high altar was erected in 1907, the reredos and surrounds being carved by Michael Pearse, father of Patrick and Willie Pearse, executed leaders of the Easter Rising of 1916. The Choir Screen of 1921 makes a beautiful entrance to the choir and chancel, but in the absence of the designer was erected back to front! Bronze railings and gates were added in 1929, and to commemorate the 800th anniversary of the Cathedral, the oak sanctuary doors were installed in 1968.

St Mary's Cathedral abounds in medieval and later tombs, memorials, and mural tablets. Of historic interest is the Earls of Thomond Memorial, which occupies a large Gothic arch on the north wall between chancel and sacristy. As part of a policy of Surrender and Regrant introduced by Henry VIII, Irish chieftains who surrendered their lands and titles to the king received them back with promises of protection under English law and titles of English nobility. Many chieftains surrendered, including the O'Briens whose head Murrough became Earl of Thomond and Baron of Inchiquin. The lower effigy is that of Donogh O'Brien, fourth Earl of Thomond, who died in 1624. On the tier above that is an effigy of Elizabeth Fitzgerald, wife of Donogh. At the base is the stone coffin lid of Donal Mór O'Brien (+1194), the founder of Limerick Cathedral. It is the oldest monument in the Church. The oblong-shaped lid is set into a black marble frame. It is ornamented with a ringed cross, and bears the three lions of the O'Brien arms.

Romanesque Doorway

Another Murrough O'Brien, first Earl of Inchiquin, took the Protestant side in the struggle between Charles I and Parliament and against the Catholic Confederate Army which supported the king. Later in the war he changed sides and was pronounced a traitor. At the funeral of this notorious political opportunist in 1674 his body was forcibly taken from St Mary's and thrown into the River Shannon. The empty coffin was unearthed 200 years later and reburied in the O'Brien Chapel; the spot had been marked by the single letter *I* – meaning Inchiquin – cut into the pavement.

In the St James Chapel, the Galwey-Bultingfort-Stritch Memorial dating from after 1400 is an excellent example of typical fifteenth-century monumental sculpture. It is surmounted by a heavily moulded triangular pediment. Crockets are carved in high relief all along its upper edges and there is a richly carved finial at the top. The cinque-foiled arch is supported on short octagonal piers. Slim, vertical pilasters frame the tomb, with angels carved at the base and decorated finials on top. The stone altar in this chapel is pre-Reformation in date. Above the altar the Westropp Memorial depicts three scenes from the Passion and Resurrection of Christ. An antiquary of note, Thomas Johnson Westropp was the son of Anne Westropp, benefactor of the 1862 restoration of the south transept. Westropp died in 1839 – later, on his mother's death, his coffin was opened and found empty! The sedilia in the south wall has trefoil arches resting on spiral-fluted shafts and dates from 1400.

The choir stalls of a church do not usually call for much comment, but in Limerick Cathedral these stalls, known as misericords, of rare occurrence and the only medieval example in Ireland, are the most interesting of the church furnishings. Carved out of black oak they date from about 1490. The seat of the misericord was made to tip up so that a tired clergyman could lean back for a rest against a ledge fitted to the underside. In the process of time the undersides were decorated with carved motifs that included humans, animals, and birds. Recognisable animals at St Mary's are the antelope (whose horns symbolise the Old and New Testaments), the lion, and the wild boar. There is a swan, symbol of the martyrs, and an eagle – also an angel. There is also a liberal representation of mythical creatures: cockatrice

Misericords in St Mary's

(a two-headed lizard), manticora (with human face, lion's body, eagle's wings, and scorpion's tail), wyvern (a two-legged dragon), lindworm (a wingless wyvern), and griffin (a quadruped with the forepart of an eagle and the hindquarters of a lion).

Concluding on the human level, the visitor will be hard pressed not to spend time browsing around old churchyards like St Mary's, where memorable scraps of wit and wisdom are to be gleaned from the doggerel on the crumbling grave slabs:

> Here lieth little Samuel Barrington that great undertaker,
> Of famous cittis clock and chime maker,
> He made his one (own) time go early and latter (later),
> But now he is returned to God his Creator.

Location: Nicholas Street. Open year-round.

CHRIST CHURCH CATHEDRAL
Dublin, County Dublin

The Cathedral of the Holy Trinity, generally known as Christ Church, is the earlier of the two medieval cathedrals of Dublin. The story begins with a cathedral co-founded by the Viking king of Dublin, Sitric Silkenbeard, and Donatus, the first known bishop of Dublin. A date about 1038 is given for the consecration of this building, of which no trace now remains. Viking allegiance kept Silkenbeard's Cathedral under the See of Canterbury until 1152, when it became independent. One decade later Laurence O'Toole, now St Laurence O'Toole, patron saint of Dublin, became Archbishop of Dublin. Under his jurisdiction the Canons Regular of St Augustine were given charge of the Cathedral. One decade later again, the Anglo-Normans were in control of Dublin and the construction of a new cathedral was begun, a building that represents the beginning of English styles in Ireland, and the gradual supplanting of native ones. Work continued under John Comyn, Archbishop of Dublin from 1181, being finally completed about 1240.

The prestige and pageantry of the consecration of archbishops were enjoyed by Christ Church, and it was at Christ Church that the highest representatives of the Crown took their oaths of office and accepted the Sword of State. In 1395, the Cathedral witnessed the knighting by Richard II of four Irish princes – and on one memorable Sunday in 1487, the coronation of a king. On that occasion, the ten year-old Lambert Simnel, pretender to the English throne, was crowned King of England and Lord of Ireland by the Archbishop of Dublin. Fifty years later the Chapter of Christ Church was secularised as part of the suppression of the Irish monasteries under Henry VIII. Since then it has remained a Protestant house of worship, and since the disestablishment of the Church of Ireland in 1869, as the Cathedral of the Protestant Diocese of Dublin.

In its original form Christ Church was an amalgam of two successive architectural styles, the Late Romanesque of the choir and transepts dating from just before 1200, and the Early English Gothic of the nave which was begun about 1210 and completed about 1235. Fortunately, sufficient remains of both styles to enable the visitor to savour the Transitional character of the architecture.

Christ Church had its due share of misfortunes. As early as 1283 the chapter house, dormitory, and cloister of the Canons Regular were destroyed in a fire that took the Cathedral tower as well. In 1316 the belfry tower was again blown down in a storm. The worst disaster occurred in 1562 when the nave ceiling collapsed carrying with it the Cathedral roof and the south wall of the nave. A wooden roof was then erected and the south arcade replaced by a blank wall.

Throughout the 1870s a major rebuilding of the Cathedral was entrusted to the Victorian architect George Street of London, hired and financially supported by a wealthy Dublin benefactor, Henry Roe, who donated a princely quarter of a million pounds, and ended up bankrupt. Street was one of the leading authorities on medieval architecture of the day. He rebuilt the south wall of the nave to match the north wall, replaced the nave vaulting, and attempted to restore the choir to its original twelfth-century Romanesque appearance. For the new tiled floor more than 60 patterns from some thirteenth-century tiles were used. The only remaining parts of the original church are the transepts, the north wall of the nave, and the crypt.

On entering Christ Church one is at once struck by the grandeur of the nave walls. Viewed from the choir the north arcade is seen to lean noticeably outward. Each nave wall is divided in half along its length by a horizontal string-course that separates the nave arcade from the triforium and clerestory levels. The deeply cut mouldings of the arches and pillars of the arcade are of rich effect, each pillar a cluster of eight banded circular shafts, alternating with eight small filleted rolls in pairs, and surmounted by foliage-scroll capitals with heads that peer out from the corners. The central shafts continue on up to the springing of the vaulting ribs. Unsurpassed elsewhere in Irish building the plan is special to Christ Church. In each bay the three pointed arches of each of the triforium and clerestory levels form one unit framed by a pointed arch, a unity accentuated by banded marble shafts that continue up through both storeys.

The twelfth-century transepts are among the earliest products of Anglo-Norman ecclesiastical work in Ireland. There is a confusing mix of pointed arches and round arches featuring chevron ornamentation, and the triforium and clerestory archways are jammed together. Capitals in the north transept have Romanesque animal and figure scenes – one shows a group of musicians, another has four dragons entwined around two human busts. Elsewhere in the Cathedral the capitals feature mainly foliage designs.

As cathedrals go, Christ Church is strikingly lacking in monuments. One reason is that many memorials that formerly graced the Church were transferred to the crypt during the 1870s restoration. The Strongbow monument in the south aisle of the nave remained untouched. In August 1170 the Anglo-Norman knight Richard de Clare, Earl of Pembroke, usually known as Strongbow, came to Ireland. Eight months later, on the death of Dermot MacMurrough, whose daughter Eva he had married, he became the designated heir to the Kingdom of Leinster. It was Strongbow who aided Archbishop Laurence O'Toole in founding the second cathedral of Christ Church in 1172. He was buried in the Cathedral in 1176 close to the present Strongbow monument. The small effigy alongside is believed to be a trimmed version of the actual Strongbow tomb broken in the ceiling collapse of 1562, and the existing Strongbow tomb is not the original. The memorial to St Laurence O'Toole is a heart-shaped iron box containing the saint's heart, now attached to the wall of the Chapel of St Laud.

The crypt, extending the whole length of the building, is the only one of its kind in Ireland and England, and its great forest of pillars and groin-vaulted arches carries the weight of the building. Preserved in the crypt are the 1670 Stocks of the

The Crypt

Liberty of the Cathedral, the tabernacle and pewter candlesticks said to have been used for Mass during a visit by James II in 1689, and miscellaneous other statues and memorials of historic interest. Over the centuries the crypt was used for religious services, and for burials – and in the sixteenth century, during the worst days of the Cathedral, the vaults were even used as shops, and tippling rooms for beer, wine, and tobacco.

Location: Christ Church Place. Open daily.

HOLY CROSS ABBEY
Holy Cross, County Tipperary

A more delightful monastic setting would be hard to imagine than that of Holy Cross Abbey, embracing the west bank of the River Suir, just below the town of Thurles. And, because of its superb restoration, no other venue offers the visitor a comparable experience of a medieval abbey. Originally Benedictine, Holy Cross was colonised in 1180 from the Cistercian house at Monasteranenagh, County Limerick. The Charter was granted in 1186 by Donal Mór O'Brien, King of Thomond:

> Know you all good Christians that I have given these lands ... in fields, in woods, in pastures, meadows, waters, fisheries and mills, wholly, entirely, freely, and peacefully to the monks of Holy Cross.

To Donal Mór also is given the credit for donating the relic of the True Cross from which the Abbey gets its name. The resulting veneration enjoyed by Holy Cross as a place of pilgrimage earned it a major fifteenth-century restoration extending from about 1430 to 1500. This is the structure that mainly underlies the restoration of the 1970s and 1980s.

In the period between the foundation and dissolution of Holy Cross, the monks survived on income from granges that were partly worked and partly leased, and of which sheep farming and the development of fisheries were large components. In 1536 and 1539 Acts of Suppression to dissolve monastic foundations were passed by Henry VIII. Holy Cross forestalled dissolution by becoming, in 1534, a secular college controlled by a layman provost. The Abbey along with its property finally went to Black Tom, 10th Earl of Ormond, in 1561, but the monks did maintain some presence there until about 1750.

Entering the church through the reconstructed twelfth-

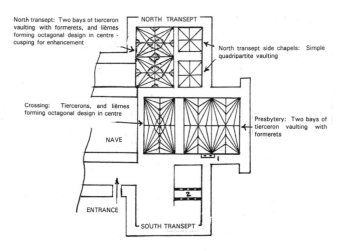

Holy Cross Abbey Vaulting

century Processional Doorway, the eye is immediately arrested by the lavish display of medieval vaulting that covers the presbytery, crossing, north transept, and the side chapels of both transepts. Cistercian austerity here gives way to Ormond patronage, notably that of James Butler, the fourth Earl, who died in 1462. There is a progressive increase in complexity. The north transept side chapels have simple quadripartite vaults. The two-bayed presbytery vault features tiercerons. Lièrnes are added in the crossing, to form a central octagonal design. In the north transept the combined effect of tiercerons and lièrnes is enhanced by cusping. A graceful feature of Irish vaulting as exemplified in Holy Cross is the manner in which rib clusters merge to a point as they taper down into the walls, without supporting piers to ground level.

The vaulting designs of the ceilings of Holy Cross remind the observer of the persistence of the outdated fourteenth-century English Decorated style in a fifteenth-century Irish restoration. Contact with English models had been broken by the Black Death of 1348. The variety of window tracery patterns used displays the same lack of direction and harking back to older models as is evidenced by the wide choice of ceiling patterns.

Nevertheless, ceilings and windows are alive with decorative effects against which the severity of the nave architecture stands contrasted. The north arcade of the nave with its plain rubble pillars and pointed arches survives from the original twelfth-century building. The fifteenth-century restorers were content to match it on the south side. Halfway down the nave the high wall with pointed arch marks the point of separation of the monks' choir from that of the lay brothers.

Altogether the finest product of medieval stone sculpture in Ireland is the sedilia in the centre of the south wall of the presbytery. This tall structure is carved out of highly durable blue-grey limestone. The area below the seats is divided into seven similar panels showing a leaf design. The seats are separated by slender octagonal pillars surmounted by three ogee arches, the effect marred by the broken cusping below the arches. Large vine-leaf crockets decorate the upper curves of the arches. Between the arches are carvings of five shields, two of them charged with the Arms of England and Ormond. The six niches above the shields are decorated with stylised foliage patterns that are again repeated above the scalloped edge of the canopy frontal that sets off the structure at the top. For good measure, the recesses under the arches and canopy are decorated with magnificent small-scale rib vaults.

Doubling as a separating wall between the side chapels of the south transept and a support for their arches and rib vaults is an enigmatic feature called The Monks' Waking Place', whose true function is not known. Was it a shrine for the relic of the True Cross? a tomb? or, indeed, a waking place for deceased monks? More than likely it was a shrine before which departed brethren were waked. The structure is of limestone and has three pointed arches on each side that rise out of spirally fluted columns that continue straight up into the moulding of the arches. The columns stand over a low wall on each side ornamented with a line of 14 ogee arches

Chapter House, Parlour and Slype

and foliated pinnacles similar to those on the sedilia in the presbytery. A beautifully carved miniature ribbed vault in three bays forms the ceiling behind the side arches.

On the crossing piers and elsewhere, about 20 masons' marks are cut into the masonry, using designs that include interlace and floral motifs. These little sculptures were the identifying trademarks of medieval professional masons. Their precise function is not known, but one can conjecture that they measured performance (for the purpose of payment or quality control) and, on occasion, may have been prestige symbols. Whatever their purpose, they add a wonderful human touch to the cold stonework.

In the north-west corner of the north transept a badly disfigured wall painting depicts a hunting scene in discernible colours of black, green, red, and brown. It probably dates from after 1500. Three hunters are shown, two with bows and

Monks' Waking Place

arrows, the third, in hooded cap and pleated skirt, blowing a
horn and holding a dog on a leash, while the stag crouches
behind an oak tree. The presence of a hunting scene on a

Cistercian church wall may appear out of context, but this popular medieval subject is depicted elsewhere (but not in Ireland) in the Cistercian environment. Monks themselves have been well known to have engaged in hunting.

The cloister arcade at Holy Cross dates from about 1450. What survives has been reassembled along the north walkway as part of the recent Abbey restoration. Enough remains to number this among the most elaborately designed of Cistercian arcades. The pointed arches are in groups of three, and richly decorated with sub-cusps. Each group is flanked by sturdy piers with raking buttresses, and the effect is most pleasing.

The barrel-vaulted chapter house is entered from the east walkway. In the Cistercian environment the chapter house was the most important monastic room, where the monks gathered daily after Mass for prayers, advice, and a reading from the Rule. Chapter house doorways were normally architecturally impressive. Only at Holy Cross does the billet-ornamented doorway survive intact, but it is not an outstanding example.

Between 1142 and 1300 the Cistercians built about 40 Irish abbeys, ruins of only about half of which remain. Conservation has necessarily been very selective, and restorations even more so. At Duiske Abbey in Graignamanagh, County Kilkenny, at least the church was restored. The measure of restoration accorded to Holy Cross makes it indeed a privileged place.

Location: Holy Cross, 4m (6.5km) south of Thurles. Open daily.

St Flannan's Cathedral
Killaloe, County Clare

Beautifully situated on the west bank of the River Shannon just below Lough Derg, the Cathedral Church of St Flannan is among the earliest and most attractive of Irish cathedrals, its attraction lying in the fact that it is a simple medieval church that has somehow managed to retain much of its original appearance and atmosphere.

Killaloe was once the capital of the Dalcassian Kingdom of the powerful O'Brien dynasty. St Flannan was a seventh-century prince of the Dalcassians and ancestor of the illustrious High King Brian Ború, who routed the Vikings at the Battle of Clontarf in 1014. The present Transitional cathedral was begun about 1185 by Donal Mór O'Brien, King of Thomond, and, after some interim destruction, brought to near completion by Donal's successor Murtagh who died in 1220. Right up to the seventeenth century the historical record is quite scant, but it is known that, after some intense initial wrangling between Irish and Anglo-Normans, only Irishmen occupied the see and chapter of Killaloe until after the Reformation.

Killaloe Cathedral is of cruciform shape, comprising aisleless nave, chancel, transepts, and a square tower placed centrally over the crossing. The purple and yellow sandstone exterior is plain and unpretentious. Most noteworthy among the external features is the early triplet of graceful lancet windows in the east gable of the chancel, exhibiting Transitional character in the combination of window shapes (two pointed and one round-arched) and the separation of the lights by narrow walls rather than mullions. One might say that little has changed, except that the tower has been altered considerably. Before 1800 it was low, and surmounted by a quaint pyramid-shaped roof set off with a weather vane. By about 1890 it had acquired its present height along with Irish-style stepped battlements and corner turrets.

An 1843 description of the nave as 'a large, void and naked place not used for Service' is a pointer to the poor days on which the Cathedral had fallen. Some 40 years later the fate of the nave was finally sealed by the erection of a huge Gothic oak screen that separated it from the remaining parts of the church. Whereas the purpose of the screen was the laudable one of heat conservation, it badly restricts the general view of the interior. The now disused nave is poorly lit by just two lancets in each of the north and south walls and a single lancet over the west entrance doorway. The visitor who has seen St Laserian's in Old Leighlin cannot but be struck by the similarity between the thirteenth-century whitewashed walls and flagged floors of the naves of both churches.

Chevrons, grotesque beasts, human heads, and foliage designs are carved into the recessed Romanesque doorway with hood moulding and four orders, located at the west end of the south nave wall. A possible survival from Donal Mór's earlier cathedral, tradition has this great doorway, which rivals that of Clonfert, located over the cross-inscribed tomb slab of Murtagh O'Brien (+1119), great-grandson of Brian Ború, and last of the Dalcassian High Kings, the one who in 1101 had generously donated the Rock of Cashel to the Irish Church. Against the west wall is a twelfth-century High Cross that originally stood in the churchyard of Kilfenora Cathedral, County Clare; a Crucifixion scene is accompanied with interlacing and fret designs. Close by is an Ogham stone bearing a rare Viking Runic inscription.

Stained glass depicting Christ surrounded by the Twelve Apostles fills the Transitional lancet windows of the east chancel wall, and is highlighted by the stark whiteness of the chancel walls; one is reminded that lime-washing of church walls was a medieval practice.

Well-dressed as it is by comparison with the nave, the whole church east of the dividing screen exhibits a simplicity that makes detailed description unnecessary. It is an important ingredient of the charm of Ireland's church heritage that so many of the older cathedrals, like Killaloe, make no pretence of ostentatious style or size or architectural grandeur. As elsewhere, the return from Killaloe consists in catching the spirit of the place. Beyond noting its few highlights, it consists in observing a selection of simpler things like the yellow sandstone medieval baptismal font, the simple quadripartite vault supporting the tower, the quaint kilted figures and other carvings on the corbels along the side walls of the chancel. And it can include a reflection on things that have gone, like the stern judgments once meted out to sinners in the Bishop's Court that occupied the chapel of the former south transept.

In the Cathedral grounds stands the twelfth-century St Flannan's Oratory, its date prompted by its Romanesque doorway and the fact that it had a chancel (now gone) from the beginning. It is of construction broadly similar to that of St Kevin's Church in Glendalough – steep stone corbelled roof supported on the interior by the arch of the barrel vault, aided by the pointed corbelled vault of the croft above it. The west end Romanesque doorway is of three orders of round arches. Discernible on the rather worn capitals are carvings of two animals and some stylised foliage. As one of just a handful of such stone-roofed ancient Irish churches remaining, St Flannan's Oratory is a monument of very special value.

Location: Killaloe. Open daily

BALLINTUBBER ABBEY
Ballintubber, County Mayo

> In that day I will raise up the fallen dwelling-place of David, all
> its breaches made good, all its ruins restored; it shall stand once
> more as it stood long ago.

Words like these from the prophecy of Amos fitly describe the
spirit of Ballintubber, the Abbey that refused to die. Founded
in 1216, partially burned in 1265, suppressed in 1542, reduced
to ruins by Cromwellian forces in 1653, gradually restored
since 1889, and continuing as the only Irish church where the
Mass has been offered without interruption for close on 800
years – the indomitable Augustinian Abbey of Ballintubber
has made good its determination to live.

The Canons Regular of St Augustine were secular priests
who lived in community according to the Rule of St
Augustine of Hippo (+430). Beyond their cloistral duties they
served in local parish churches, hospitals and schools. Like
the Cistercians from Clairvaux, they were introduced to
Ireland from the French Arroasian observance by St Malachy,
Archbishop of Armagh (1094-1148), foremost pioneer of
twelfth-century Gregorian Reform in Ireland.

Ballintubber Abbey was founded by the King of
Connaught, Cathal O'Connor 'of the wine-red hand' (from
the red birthmark on his left hand). It was advantaged by
large grants of land from royal sources, gifts from wealthy
benefactors, and rents from dependent churches and parishes.
In a seventeenth-century report, the Abbey was declared to
have owned 3000 acres of land over 25 townlands. The year of
its dissolution by Henry VIII was 1542, but the Augustinians
continued in residence there – the geographical remoteness of
western monasteries helped to postpone the day of reckoning.
Various individuals then gradually acquired an interest in the
Abbey lands. A beginning of restoration of the Abbey in 1846
was interrupted by the potato famine of 1847. By 1889 the

transepts and chancel had been re-roofed, but restoration of the nave was not completed until 1966, in celebration of the 750th anniversary of the founding of the Abbey.

The west doorway is fifteenth century. Viewed from the exterior, it is set into a moulded arch surmounted by a hood moulding of ogee outline with carved finial, and narrow pilasters extending upwards from the sides also ending in carved finials. The aisleless nave is well lit by high round-headed windows, and set off by the magnificent fifteenth-century style roof of Irish oak constructed in 1965.

Of paramount interest are the architectural features of the crossing and chancel that exemplify a particular Transitional style called the 'school of the west' found in many western establishments over the first half of the thirteenth century. Wall-shafts everywhere start at points some feet above the ground: those in the crossing are single, and taper down almost to a point; those in the chancel are in the form of tapering triple rolls. Capitals under semi-octagonal abaci combine the scallop and foliage motifs. High-relief carving is spread right across the surfaces and the discerning eye will detect dragons, and birds with necks intertwined. Carvings by the same superlative craftsman adorn several of the capitals in the Cistercian abbey of Boyle, County Roscommon. Sturdy cross and groin ribs supporting the pointed vault of the chancel are unmoulded. The east windows of the chancel are completely framed by rounded mouldings, both within and without, and hood mouldings are continued right across the wall like a string-course. Round arches with chevrons mark these windows as a carry-over from the twelfth-century Romanesque. With the Anglo-Norman invasion of Connaught in 1235, the school of the west came to an end.

The sacristy was formerly the seventeenth-century mortuary chapel of the de Burgos, a prominent Anglo-Norman family of Connaught. The stone tomb with the remains of carvings of the Apostles on the base is that of Tióbóid na Long (Theobold of the Ships), son of Ireland's famous pirate queen, Grace O'Malley. Theobold supported the English in the Battle of Kinsale (1602) against the Ulster

Ballintubber Abbey from the East

chieftains O'Neill and O'Donnell, and in 1627 he was created
First Viscount Mayo as a reward. Two years later he was
murdered outside the Abbey by one of his own kinsmen.

The fifteenth-century cloister arcades have been partially
reconstructed. It would appear that the nave originally had a
south aisle and that the cloister arcade on its northern side
was then built upon the foundations of the south wall of this
aisle. A lean-to roof stretched over from here to the south wall
of the nave, above which can still be seen traces of the original
thirteenth-century clerestory windows.

In Irish, Ballintubber means 'the townland of the well',
the well being that of St Patrick, who also built a wooden
church close to the present Abbey on his return from a vigil on
Ireland's holy mountain, Croagh Patrick. The 20-mile road
from Ballintubber to Croagh Patrick (called Tóchar Phádraig,
St Patrick's Road) is the longest surviving pilgrim path in
Ireland.

An ongoing process of restoration and renewal at
Ballintubber is intended to keep pace with the increasing

Crossing and Chancel, Ballintubber Abbey

numbers who annually visit this great symbol of Ireland's monastic heritage.

Just south of Ballintubber is the ruined Augustinian

Abbey of Cong, with its exquisitely carved doorways, one Romanesque and one Transitional, and its partially reconstructed cloister.

Location: About 12m (19km) south of Castlebar off the N84. Open daily.

ST DOULAGH'S CHURCH
Balgriffin, County Dublin

> We, therefore, do hereby declare our will and pleasure that, with
> a view to enlarging the boundaries of the church, restraining the
> downward course of vice ... and for the increase of the Christian
> religion, you shall enter that island and execute what may tend
> to the honour of God and the welfare of the land ...

The papal Bull *Laudabiliter* given to Henry II by Pope
Adrian IV was a mandate for the Anglo-Norman conquest of
Ireland, within two years of which, in 1171, Leinster was in
the hands of the invader, and remained an area of direct
English rule radiating from Dublin. The little early thirteenth-
century church of St Doulagh (doo-lock), just north of the city,
is a rare surviving link with that time, when the 'obedient
English' were given the opportunity of worshipping in the
well-appointed new parish churches of the towns and
villages, while the 'Irish enemy' continued to use the more
primitive stone Celtic churches whose ruins still dot the
countryside. Further Papal Bulls of 1179 and 1186 assigned St
Doulagh's to the Dublin Cathedral of Christ Church, to be
administered by the Canons Regular of St Augustine.

When the present church was duly built to serve the local
parish of Balgriffin, it was set up as a small monastery, but it
included an anchorite's cell. Whether it was the Canons or
another group of monks or priests who resided at St
Doulagh's is not certain, but arrangements for inclusion of a
recluse derived from the fact that St Doulagh himself was a
seventh-century hermit, who is also described as Bishop and
Confessor, suggesting that he may have acted in the role of
both hermit and pastor. In any event, the eremitical tradition
at St Doulagh's did persist, because as late as 1406 the
chaplain of St Doulagh's was described as an anchorite.

The old St Doulagh's is an antique gem, a small oblong
building with a low square tower in the centre – the upper

St Doulagh's Church

part a fifteenth-century addition – an exceptionally steeply pitched roof of wrought stone on each side of the tower, supported along its interior by the pointed vault of an attic room. At ground floor level there is an Oratory on the east side, and a Prior's Chamber over a Hermit's Cell on the west. The first floor is a long narrow room made up of an east end Refectory and west end Dormitory. Four steps across the width of the room lead to the Dormitory that only has floor space sufficient for a few monks lying on straw beds. The fireplace may have added some comfort to this austere spot. One further upper room in the Tower is called the Library. The different levels are reached by dark narrow spiral stairways, negotiated with the aid of ropes!

The Oratory is now the Church of Ireland vestry. Two apertures in the south wall are known as lepers' windows; in an area where leprosy was once common, Holy Communion was passed out through these to the lepers outside. There is a hole low down in the west wall through which persons with head ailments pushed their heads in hopes of a cure. Late nineteenth-century excavation of the Oratory floor exposed some skeletal remains: the floor is now flagged and at a much higher level than it was originally.

The mass of masonry against the east wall of the adjacent Hermit's Cell is known as the tomb of St Doulagh. In one wall of the cell a small aperture with a triangular arch is known as the Confessional Opening. If the anchorite sat on the stairs leading up to the Prior's Chamber, he could hear the confessions of penitents entering and leaving by the south door. The extra ceiling space required for the Prior's Chamber was acquired by raising the floor of the overhead attic room at the west end. From his stone seat in the west wall the Prior could see through a window in the north wall so angled as to give a view of the Baptistry in the field beyond. The Baptistry is a stone-roofed octagonal building with steps that lead down to St Doulagh's Well, and is unique in Ireland in being the only baptistry remaining detached from the church.

A stairway leads from the Prior's Chamber to the upper tower room, the Library. Opening off this stairway is a small chamber in the wall, too small for a person to fully either lie down or sit up in, and therefore thought to have been a Penitent's Bed. With just a tiny window for light, it would have provided a fine measure of discomfort at short order. The Library – now the belfry – was a cosy room with five windows and a fireplace. Corbel stones set into the east and west walls formerly supported a wooden spire rising out of the tower.

The fine Church of Ireland building on the north side of the old church was consecrated in 1865 and is a replacement of various structures that previously stood on the same site.

Location: Dublin Road R107 about 3m (5km) from Malahide. Guided tours on Sundays 15.00 to 17.00 May to September.

ST CANICE'S CATHEDRAL
Kilkenny, County Kilkenny

St Canice was born in County Derry about 525. He founded a number of churches, the principal one being Aghaboe in County Laois. There is no evidence that he ever founded a church in Kilkenny, but when Kilkenny replaced Aghaboe as the episcopal seat of the Ossory diocese about 1200, his name became associated with Kilkenny, of where he is now the patron saint.

St Canice's is the fifth, and second largest, of Irish medieval cathedrals. Previous building on the site included at least a Round Tower, a wooden church destroyed by fire about 1087, and a Romanesque stone church which occupied the east end of the present cathedral site. The Round Tower remains intact except for its conical cap, and can be climbed to the top by a series of ladders. Carry a handbell for authenticity!

St Canice's is a powerful symbol of the move from the monastic to the episcopal system that resulted from the combined effect of twelfth-century church reforms and the Anglo-Norman conquest. Noble patronage joined forces with episcopal zeal in the spate of church building that coincided with the peak of that conquest. St Canice's is a product of that zeal, and even if building began under Hugh de Rous (+1218), Ossory's first Anglo-Norman bishop, the title 'first founder' has been bestowed on Hugh de Mapilton, who was Bishop of Ossory from 1251 to 1260, and credit for completion of the work to his successor Geoffrey St Leger, who died in 1287. Then comes a piece of tragi-comedy from local history. In 1324 Dame Alice Kyteler, Kilkenny's notorious witch, was charged with sorcery. She was duly convicted along with her son William Outlaw and her maid Petronella. Alice escaped, but Petronella was burned at the stake, and Outlaw was required to re-roof part of the Cathedral with lead. That was done – but in 1332 it all collapsed with the weight!

St Canice's has been Church of Ireland since the

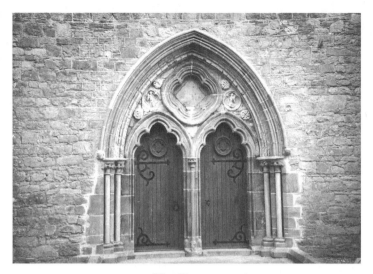

West Doorway

Reformation, except for a short period of the Confederate War of the 1640s when native Catholic Irish and Old English (Anglo-Norman stock) united on the side of royalty in the war between King and Parliament in England. In 1650 Cromwell occupied Kilkenny and attempted to destroy the Cathedral by removing the roof.

Early English largely describes the architectural style of St Canice's, but its exterior gives rather the impression of massive Romanesque solidity than of the fragile airy lightness of Gothic, the walls and squat tower with Irish-style stepped parapets, an addition to many church buildings from the fourteenth century on. Its finest external feature is the old west doorway, which has two openings with pointed cinque-foiled arches. A heavily moulded pointed arch carried on pairs of nook-shafts embraces both openings, and the spandrel between this arch and those of the openings has a large quatrefoil in the centre, also heavily moulded, and worn circular carvings on each side. This Early English use of the geometric forms of circles and foiled shapes points the way towards the introduction of tracery.

One must move inside to appreciate the uncluttered simplicity, spaciousness, and consistent imprint of the Early English design – Early English throughout all its development, and relatively unaffected by later restorations. Limestone preponderates, with sandstone dressings confined to the east (earliest) end of the Church. The three tall pointed graduated east end windows are separated by wall spaces on the exterior – separation of lancets by mullions only was a later development. But because of the splay, the window openings merge together on the interior, where the inner embrasures are framed by banded marble shafts with stiff-leaf foliage capitals based on stylised trefoil leaves, and the rear arches have dogtooth decoration – all in the typical thirteenth-century Early English manner. Similar triplets of lancets, but round-headed and with trefoiled rear arches, are set into the north and south walls of the sanctuary. The nave arcade is five-bayed, its partly moulded pointed arches of two orders carried on unusually widely spaced pillars of quatrefoil section with moulded capitals, the first such pillars introduced into Ireland. Clerestory windows are placed over the arches, quatrefoil on the exterior, and deeply inset on the interior in a concern for generous lighting supplemented by the nine lancet windows surrounding the sanctuary. Inoffensive departures from the style are the fifteenth-century lièrne vaulted roof over the crossing, designed to reinforce the tower supports after the collapse of 1332, and the magnificent hammer-beam roofs (unusual for Ireland) of the nave and transepts, which were part of a major restoration of the 1860s conducted by Sir Thomas Newenham Deane. The question of a timber roof as such was not the issue, since St Canice's, like all Irish medieval cathedrals, had never opted for a stone-vaulted interior, a decision that permitted the wide inter-columniation in the nave noted above. Deane, son of a noted Cork architect, was in the forefront of the nineteenth-century neo-Gothic movement. He may have formally offended against thirteenth-century medieval practice by removing the whitewashed plaster from the interior walls, but in the process they acquired a new and special beauty.

Interior of St Canice's

An unusual feature of interest is the confined gallery over the west doorway, perhaps a platform from which was heralded the grand arrival of the bishop on ceremonial occasions.

The choir stalls of Danubian oak were carved at Bruges in 1904, and the panels depict scenes of Irish church interest. In one, St Patrick is shown addressing an Irish chief at Tara on Easter morning; in another, St Canice instructs the people of the district near his cell.

St Canice's Cathedral is a treasure-house of monumental and funerary sculpture. Effigial tombs of sixteenth-century date claim most of the attention, but there are also floor slabs commemorating prominent personages, and miscellaneous other memorabilia. From medieval times it was the custom for wealthy individuals to commission tombs or memorials for themselves or their families, sometimes years before they died, leaving space for an inscription and a date to be filled in. When the Archbishop of Cashel commissioned the illustrious Peter Scheemakers to do a mural for his wife Anna Cox (+1745) and left a blank for his own inscription, it prompted one wag to suggest that the Archbishop's life was indeed best expressed by just that! But he *did* get his inscription, and date of death – 1779.

The finest monument is the tomb of Piers Rua Butler (+1539) and his wife Margaret Fitzgerald; theirs was a union of the Earldoms of Ormond and Kildare in the heady days when the Crown found itself forced to depend on the great Irish Earls to govern Ireland. The finely carved effigies are magnificent. Carvings on the surround of this and other tombs are of the Apostles, at least some of them the work of the famous sixteenth-century tomb sculptors Rory and William O'Tunney. The Apostles carry the insignia by which they are usually depicted in art, in some cases the instruments of their martyrdom. A floor slab close to the entrance porch is carved with the instruments of Christ's Passion, a common motif; others are of special interest because they show the trade emblems of the deceased – carpenter, weaver, shoemaker. The oldest tomb in St Canice's (in the north transept) is thought to be that of one or other of the first two builders of the Cathedral, Hugh de Mapilton or Geoffrey St Leger, and probably the former. Possibly the best thirteenth-century tomb niche in Ireland, it has a strongly moulded trefoiled arch, carved heads as stops to the hood-moulding, and dog-tooth ornament beside the supporting nook-shafts. Beside it is St Kieran's Chair in which the Bishops of Ossory continue to be enthroned. And there is the oldest inscribed tomb slab in

St Canice's Cathedral

the Cathedral, that of Jose de Keteller (+1280), father of Kilkenny's famous witch, Alice.

Just east of Kilkenny city stands the ruined Anglo-Norman parish church of Gowran, a rare and precious thirteenth-century survival. Similarity in the architectural detail gives Gowran an unmistakable likeness to St Canice's. Two other Anglo-Norman town parish churches of enduring interest are the early thirteenth-century St Multose Church in Kinsale, and St Mary's Church in Youghal, both in County Cork.

Location: Irishtown. Open year-round.

SLIGO ABBEY
Sligo, County Sligo

The term 'abbey' is, of course, a misnomer. Like that of the Franciscans, the other mendicant order, a Dominican house could be correctly described as a 'friary', but the term 'priory' is also used. The Friars Preachers were already in Ireland when the Franciscans arrived in 1232, and both Orders first expanded in or in the vicinity of new Anglo-Norman towns.

The foundation of Sligo town may be fairly attributed to the Anglo-Norman Maurice Fitzgerald, whose lordship of North Connacht was in recognition of the part he played in Richard de Burgo's conquest of Connacht in 1235. By 1245 Maurice had built a castle in Sligo, and by 1252 had founded there the Dominican Friary of the Holy Cross. In the ongoing struggle with the O'Donnells of Tyrconnell (County Donegal) the castle was repeatedly burned, and in the fourteenth century the control of Sligo passed to the O'Connors, an influential Ulster Irish family that later adopted the grand name of O'Connor Sligo. It was through O'Connor influence that in 1568 the Friary, by becoming a house of secular priests, was saved from the general dissolution of the monasteries begun by Henry VIII and continued by Queen Elizabeth. In 1595, a few years before the final defeat of the Ulster Irish chieftains at the Battle of Kinsale, the Friary was occupied by English forces under George Bingham, who irreverently used some of the friary wood to construct siege equipment for an attack on Sligo Castle. During the Confederate War of the 1640s, when native Irish and Old English (Anglo-Norman stock) supported the monarchy in the English Civil War between Charles I and Parliament, the Friary was sacked by Parliamentary forces under Sir Frederick Hamilton. Those of the friars who managed to escape took refuge in their sister-house in Athenry, County Galway. Sligo Friary was finally deserted in 1760.

Surviving parts of the original thirteenth-century church

Sligo Abbey Nave

are the choir and north wall of the nave. Eight tall lancet
windows with sandstone dressings are set along the south
wall of the choir. Three further lancet windows in the east

wall of the choir were replaced in the fifteenth-century by the existing four-light reticulated window. The observer will note the rows of square holes that punctuate the exterior wall spaces between the eight south wall lancets. These are the put-log holes, a common ingredient of old monastic walls, into which squared-off beams were set as scaffolding supports during building. When the building was completed, the beams were either removed or sawn off close to the wall and allowed to rot.

Other fifteenth-century items of interest in the church are the altar, and the rood screen set against the west wall of the tower. Plain medieval high altars remain, but, with its frontage of carved ogee-headed panels, the high altar of Sligo Friary is the sole surviving sculptured example in Ireland. The rood screen, partially reassembled (there is a similar, near-perfect example at Clontuskert, County Galway), consisted of a platform about 7feet (2m) wide set on two parallel rows of three pointed arches supported by octagonal pillars and ribbed vaulting. On the platform stood a large wooden Crucifixion scene. That was the Dominican model and was usually in wood; in the Franciscan scheme of things, a rood loft was set directly into the thickness of the tower walls.

A south aisle and transept may be sixteenth-century additions to the nave, but neither retains any architectural features of interest.

On the north side of the church are considerable remains of the thirteenth-century chapter house. Regrettably, its three east wall lancet windows are now blocked up. The cloisters date from the fifteenth century, and are among the finest Dominican examples in Ireland. As in the Franciscan context, they are of the integrated type, where the thick sturdy archways, aided by the bluntly pointed barrel vaults of the ambulatories, support the walls and rooms above them. Unglazed cloister arcades provided an airy, sheltered place for prayer, relaxed exercise and conversation. In Sligo Friary they are well-preserved on three sides.

In the church are two monuments of distinction. The

O'Craian Tomb

earlier one is the O'Craian (Crean) tomb of 1506, set into the north wall of the nave, its date certified by the Latin inscription on the tomb chest at the base, which dedicates the memorial to Cormac O'Craian and his wife, Johanna Ennis. In the ogee-headed niches along the tomb frontal are low-relief figure carvings: the Crucifixion in the centre, with the Virgin Mary and St John on each side; other identifiable figures are St Dominic in a friar's garb, St Peter with keys, the winged St Michael the Archangel bearing sword and shield, and St Catherine of Alexandria with sword and wheel. Remains of some fine tracery are found on the pointed canopy above the tomb.

Only the briefest description can be given of the second monument, this time a memorial of 1624 known as the O'Connor Sligo monument. This elaborate Renaissance monument occupies the east end of the south wall of the choir. At the top, the arms of O'Connor Sligo are surmounted by a crucifixion and flanked by figures arguably representing Saints Peter and Paul. Below this, round-arched niches are occupied by kneeling effigies of Sir Donogh and his wife: on the pilaster close to O'Connor are the symbols of battle; on that beside Lady Elinora, gentle symbols appropriate to womanhood that include an open book and flower. Uncompromising emblems of death – skulls, hourglass, scythe and spade – form the subject of the panel below that carrying the inscription.

Within 80 years of their establishment in Ireland, Dominican houses numbered upwards of 50. Most are now in a considerable state of ruin. Let mention be made of just two. On a level grassy sward beside a town that retains more than a share of its medieval past, the skeleton Dominican Priory of the Anglo-Norman town of Kilmallock, County Limerick, continues to convey a real sense of former grandeur. And in Kilkenny city is the Black Abbey Church of 1225 that has been restored for worship.

Location: Abbey Street, Sligo

COLLEGIATE CHURCH OF
ST NICHOLAS
Galway, County Galway

The saint in question is the fourth-century Nicholas, Bishop of Myra in Turkey, better known as Santa Claus, patron of children, sailors, unmarried girls, apothecaries, perfumiers, and pawnbrokers. With such an interesting following it is not surprising that many churches were dedicated to Nicholas – more than 400 alone in England. Not so many in Ireland, but the fourteenth-century parish Church of St Nicholas in Galway is among the finest medieval ornaments of that city. It is also the largest medieval parish church in Ireland and, among the small remaining group of these, has the distinction of being the most intact.

When the de Burgos invaded Connaught in 1235, Galway became an Anglo-Norman town, and by 1300 was walled and fortified against the hostile Irish who surrounded it on all sides. It emerged into a great medieval trading post, and it was the wealthy merchants of Galway who in 1320 built St Nicholas' Church for the colony. Such was the sense of independence fostered by the continued expansion of trade that by 1484 the citizens of Galway had been granted the right to elect their own clergy, mayor and bailiffs. In that year St Nicholas' Church became Collegiate. A Wardenship of Galway was founded, consisting of a senior clerical administrator known as the Warden, and a College of priests, some of whom were called Vicars. It lasted until about 1830.

The Church of 1320 was of cruciform plan with chancel, nave with narrow aisles, and north and south transepts. During the 100 years following the acquisition of Collegiate status, the north and south aisles were widened, creating three gables at the west end, a situation unique in Ireland. Starting with Dominick Dubh Lynch, who was mayor in 1486, the Lynches, who gave about 40 mayors to Galway, were the main contributors to the changes. James FitzStephen Lynch donated a stained glass window to the chancel in 1493 and, if the story be true, undertook in the same year to hang his own son Walter, whose alleged crime was that of stabbing to death a Spanish youth whom he jealously suspected of having an unhealthy interest in his fiancée, Agnes. The mayor was magistrate at the trial and, failing a hangman, did the job himself. A plaque in the churchyard placed above a tablet bearing a skull and crossbones purports to mark the site of the execution. The final significant structural alteration to the Church occurred in 1561 when Nicholas Lynch, grandson of the hangman mayor, lengthened the south transept.

After the dissolution of the monasteries under Henry VIII, the Collegiate status of St Nicholas' was confirmed by Charter of Edward VI, the Warden and eight Vicars becoming a corporate body with a common seal. When dispossession again threatened under Elizabeth I, the Collegiate body saved the property of the Church by leasing most of it at nominal rents and for long terms to their relatives and friends. St Nicholas' became Protestant in 1568 and has since maintained Church of Ireland services.

Perhaps because they are so unusual, the gargoyles below the stepped parapets of the south wall are the most interesting feature of the exterior. Their practical function was that of discharging rainwater from the roof. These quaint waterspouts come in a variety of carved heads, human and animal; there is an eagle, and a monkey, among others. There are three fine windows along the three-gabled west side of the Church. The central and earliest one has reticulated tracery; the other two have curvilinear tracery and date from the sixteenth-century widening of the north and south aisles.

Immediately inside the south porch is a sixteenth-century baptismal font that is still in use. Carvings on two sides of the font match the tracery of some of the older Church windows. Moving along the north aisle, the visitor will observe the late fifteenth-century freestanding Benitier (Holy Water Stoup) set on the floor in front of the Blessed Sacrament Chapel. This font was once stolen from the church and used as a stand for flowers in a local lady's garden. It was recovered, but not without some persuasion! At the door of the chapel is a strange stone furnishing, known both as a Confessional and a Lectern. One view is that it was originally a confessional moved from the Church to the College House of the Warden and Vicars, where it was used as a reader's desk, and that when the College House was demolished, it was returned to the Church. The pulpit that commemorates the last Warden of St Nicholas' is in the north-east corner of the crossing. A nearby banner displays the arms of the 14 Tribes of Galway, 14 influential Galway families – Blakes, Frenches, Joyces, Lynches, and the rest – who virtually controlled the Wardenship throughout most of its stormy existence.

Anyone looking for the original Church will find it in the chancel, the nave arcades, and the northern end of the south transept. This transept contains the most interesting of the tombs. The oldest is the Crusader's Tomb, dating from about 1300. Since it predates the Church, it is believed to have come from an earlier chapel of the Knights Templar. The carving on top is a combination of Greek cross and double-handed sword. Further along the east wall of the south transept are two tombs associated with the Lynch family. The window tomb from 1644 is that of the military leader, Stephen Lynch, and the large square tomb with floriated panels in the southeast corner is that of James Lynch, the mayor of 1493 who was alleged to have hanged his son Walter. Between the two Lynch tombs is the elaborately carved mid-sixteenth-century Joyce tomb-niche. The design, with its flamboyant tracery, flanking pilasters with finials, crocketed ogee arch, and frontal with a row of empty ogee-headed niches, occurs copiously in Gothic tomb-niches and wall-reliefs of the fifteenth and sixteenth centuries. The Joyce tomb is a late simplified copy of the magnificent tomb-niche in the north wall of the Dominican friary at Strade, County Mayo.

Kilmallock in County Limerick is yet another medieval town of Anglo-Norman origin that owes much to the Fitzgerald Earls of Desmond. The ruined shell of its thirteenth-century Collegiate Church of Saints Peter and Paul is a token of what might have befallen St Nicholas of Myra, had it too experienced the luckless fortunes of the Desmonds – a message hammered home by the realism of the 1630 cadaver monument of Maurice Fitzgerald with its incised skeleton and carvings of a coffined corpse and grave digger, and the inscription 'Ecce Finem' – Behold the End.

Location: Market Street. Open daily.

ROSS ERRILLY FRIARY
Headford, County Galway

Ruined and roofless, yet with pose reliant
Thou watchest faithful o'er the sleeping dead

Ross Errilly is the largest, best preserved, and most complete of Franciscan ruins in Ireland, and its story is one of rare perseverance in the face of adversity. Viewed in this dual architectural/historical light the Friary of Ross enjoys a special place in the Irish monastic scene. Considering the excellence of its preservation, it was said that with little more than a new roof the friars could return again to a home from which they had been seven times expelled.

The Order of Friars Minor, known as the Franciscans, came to Ireland about 1230 and by 1260 had established some 30 houses. These houses were sited near new Anglo-Norman towns for the most part, but nothing of them remains today. Surprisingly, the date of the foundation of Ross Errilly is reliably given as 1351, just in the wake of the Black Death of 1348. However, the Friary as it stands today is largely the result of building dating from 1498, the main benefactor being a local Galway family named Gannard.

Forty years later the Friary was suppressed by Henry VIII and the friars departed. The expulsion was short-lived – remoteness from the main political scene and the patronage of the de Burgo Earls of Clanricarde were the saving factors. Besides this protection, Ross Friary had acquired some 1300 acres of land over three townships; however, marvellous to relate, when an inventory of all Catholic lands and possessions was ordered by Queen Elizabeth, the extent of the Friary lands was mysteriously reduced to one acre, and its other possessions to a few buildings and a mill which could be worked only in wintertime because of shortage of water power! In 1580 the Friary was granted to Richard de Burgo, second Earl of Clanricarde, who promptly returned it to the friars. Thirty years later the friars were expelled on the orders of the Lord Deputy, and were not reinstated until 1626, the second year of the reign of Charles I, who was promising relief to Catholics in return for money assistance in his fight against Parliament. In 1656 the friars received advance warning of an imminent attack by Cromwellian forces and escaped to safety, but it took them years to undo the havoc wreaked by the savage soldiery. The Friary was emptied again in 1697 by an Act of William III of Orange *'for banishing all Papists exercising any ecclesiastical jurisdiction, and all regulars of the Popish clergy'*.

The final chapter in the history of Ross Errilly is not altogether without comedy. The friars had again returned in 1715 with the connivance of a tolerant local lord who was promptly reported as harbouring, and even supporting, the monks. The story goes that, to stave off disaster, the monks were advised to leave and with the aid of whitewash the church was disguised as a wool factory complete with handlooms and equipment. The ruse worked, and everybody was saved. But it was really the end, and the Friary was evacuated for the last time in 1753. Fifty years later it was in ruins.

It will help considerably in the appreciation of Ross Errilly to describe briefly the main features of fifteenth-century friary architecture. The basic Irish friary plan conformed to the Cistercian model: a square cloister arcade with the church on one side and the cloistral buildings on the other three. Dissimilarities reflected the different lifestyles of the two orders: the Cistercians following an enclosed life, the Franciscans preaching and ministering to the people. The church was therefore divided into nave for the lay congregation and chancel (choir) for the friars, these being separated by a tall slim tower resting on arched walls between nave and chancel. Aisles were not general, but there might be an annexe or transept on the south side. Cloisters were generally smaller because the friars were less bound to community life, and cloistral buildings were generally located north rather than south of the church.

Ross Errilly Friary

The nave of Ross is entered through a pointed doorway in the west gable. Beyond a small chantry chapel dating from 1678 is the south transept, separated from the nave by rounded arches that spring from sturdy octagonal piers. Here is a church that must have sometimes catered to large congregations coming from far and near. Above the chancel arch is the rood loft where a life-size representation of the Crucifixion faced the people. Winding stone stairs lead to the tower roof and a fine view of the Friary ruins below.

Stalls for the friars originally ran along the north and south walls of the chancel where the church offices were sung, commencing with Matins at early dawn. The high altar was against the east wall under the beautiful four-light traceried window. In keeping with Franciscan restraint the tracery is of simple switchline form – each of the three vertical mullions branching into curved intersecting bars at the top. Similar tracery is found in the two three-light windows of the south transept, a style dating in Ireland from about 1300.

The sacristy formed the ground floor of a three-storey annexe, the floor above the sacristy being a guest room, but surely for special guests, not just the rank-and-file who arrived daily in search of alms or shelter. These would have been met at the main monastic entrance to the north of the nave, and then catered to in a room on the west side.

Perhaps the most attractive feature of Ross Errilly is the perfectly preserved cloister arcade. It is of the integrated type characteristic of the later friaries – except on the south side where the arches were attached by a lean-to roof to the church wall. Because integrated arcades must perforce help support the walls above them, they had to be of exceptionally sturdy structure, a feature that has here and elsewhere contributed to their preservation. The broadly pointed chamfered arches are in groups of five, each group separated and reinforced by short sloping buttresses.

A small cloister area does not admit of much surrounding building, especially with the church wall taking up one side. So a second courtyard was built to the north and around this at the ground level are the kitchen and refectory ranges. The spacious kitchen is in the north-west corner, and the great kitchen fireplace has a large opening in the back through which the heat from burning logs was transmitted to the

Cloister Arcade

East Window

ovens in the adjacent bakehouse. In the north-east corner a large circular fish tank, still intact, is sunk into the floor. Fish were kept alive in the tank until needed, fresh water being fed

The Fish Tank

through the mill just north of the kitchen. Everything remains suspended in time, with the ghost of the friar kitchener standing nearby!

The chapter room was over the bakehouse. Franciscans appear not to have given as much prominence to this part of the monastic layout as did Cistercians, but the chapter room at Ross was important enough to have been the scene of several General Chapters of the Order. A particular ceremony of interest conducted in the chapter room was the triennial election of the Guardian, the Franciscan counterpart of the Cistercian Abbot.

The refectory at the east end of the north range was lighted by four mullioned windows whose widely splayed interiors distributed the light across the room. Meals were served on long heavy wooden tables and eaten in silence while the reader read from Scripture or other spiritual books. The reader's seat survives intact in a recessed area at the north-east corner. Only the unadorned rectangular windows remain of the monks' dormitory that was located over the refectory. There were no separate cells here, just rows of beds consisting of planks covered with mats.

Ross Errilly is exceptional, but not the only interesting ruined Franciscan house. Rosserk in County Mayo is compact but well preserved, and the only complete Third Order friary remaining. Further south are the friaries of Ennis and Quin in County Clare, Ennis being among the earliest foundations, and Quin unique in that it was built within the walls of an Anglo- Norman castle.

Location: 1m (2.5km) northwest of Headford. Direct access.

QUIN ABBEY
Quin, County Clare

Travelling south from Ennis to see places of historic interest, one cannot fail to be attracted to the ruins of Quin Abbey that lie just outside the pretty little village of Quin. Being a Franciscan foundation, Quin is, properly, a 'friary' but the term 'abbey' seems to be tenacious. Quin is the strange case of a friary incorporated into the square keep of an Anglo-Norman castle. It was in 1276 that Edward I granted the whole land of Thomond (County Clare) to the adventurer Thomas de Clare, who promptly invaded it and built a castle at Quin. This castle was destroyed in 1286 by the MacNamaras in reprisal for the slaughter of a local Irish chieftain, and the MacNamaras later gave the dismantled fortress to the Franciscans. Parts of the church date from the early fourteenth century but the Friary was largely rebuilt after 1400 by Síoda Cam MacNamara, chief of Clancullen. By 1433 the Observant Franciscans came to Quin under the patronage of another MacNamara, name of Maccon. The term 'Observant' applies to those Franciscan houses that adhered to the pristine ideals of poverty promoted by St Francis, as opposed to the 'Conventuals' who advocated realistic ownership and administration of property – a difference which was the cause of a century of unhappy discord within the Order.

Quin was formally dissolved by Henry VIII in 1541; it was given to the Irish Lord of Ibracken, Conor O'Brien, who kept the friars in residence. A report of the period states that the rather rundown Friary consisted of '... one great church, covered with slate, and a steeple, greatly decayed, a churchyard and cloister, one great hall, four chambers, two cellars, a ruinous dortor (dormitory) ... also one watermill, ruinous and prostrate'. Even with that poor offering the Crown disapproved of the O'Briens conniving with local Irish priests and rebels – to make good the point, Sir John Perrot, the Queen's Deputy, occupied the Abbey in 1584 and ordered that Turlough O'Brien be half hanged from a cart, his bones shattered with the back of an axe, and his body hung from the steeple of Quin. In spite of interim expulsions, the friars maintained some presence at Quin throughout the seventeenth and eighteenth centuries. The last monk, John Hogan, died in 1820 – his inscribed tombstone is in the north-east corner of the cloister.

The plan of Quin Friary is one that is roughly common to many Franciscan friaries in Ireland – a nave entered from the west with transept opening off to the south, a chancel on the east side separated from the nave by a central tower, and the claustral buildings set around the cloisters on the north side. In the case of Quin, the initial interest might be in the matter of conversion of a castle to an abbey. The castle of de Clare was a square ward enclosed by high ten feet thick curtain walls fortified by great circular corner bastions. Some of this supplied building stones for the Friary walls, but the best surviving evidence is seen in the south walls of the chancel and nave. The old castle gateway remains as part of the southern abutment of the tower, and the three windows along the south wall of the chancel are set into the thickness of the massive walls and then widely splayed both inwards and outwards. Not much remains of the corner turrets, but the lower part of the bastion at the north-east angle is well preserved; it is best viewed from an upper floor at the north end. Five altars remain intact – the high altar at the east end of the chancel, two at the east end of the nave, and two along the east wall of the transept. The east wall of the castle was adapted to accommodate the three-light chancel window; it is of early switchline tracery type with three bracing ogee arched heads linked across the top of the mullions.

The integrated arcades of the cloisters are well preserved and are among the finest of Franciscan type in Ireland, and the cloister garth is almost square. The pillars of the surrounding arcades are octagonal in shape and of the 'dumbbell' type; that is, with one at the front and one at the back joined by a web. Between each pair of openings there is a raking buttress, rather like a long slim triangular wedge that fades into the walls above the cloister arches. These buttresses were designed to counteract the outward thrust of the pointed barrel vaulted cloister walkways; in Quin they also served an aesthetic function by breaking up the monotony of the plain upper walls. Barrel vaulting was widely used from at least the twelfth century to cover ground floor rooms of various kinds. A wickerwork matting, held in place by temporary timber scaffolding (centering), first covered the intended ceiling area. Archstones were then laid across the mat and held in place by lime mortar. The wickerwork and scaffolding were removed when the mortar was set. In many cases – as at Quin – the lines of the wickerwork matting can still be seen. A person peering through the openings in the iron door of the vault of the Lords Dunboyne at the north end of the west cloister walkway will see the rather eerie-looking tiers of coffins set along the opposite walls.

To the north of the cloister the barrel vaulted range consisted of a kitchen with large fireplace to the west side and refectory to the east. The strange little corner at the west end (with the two sets of steps running up to the three-light window) is actually cut out of the thickness of the north-west bastion of the de Clare castle. Corbels set along the north and south walls of the refectory suggest that a wooden ceiling was built under the vault. Also barrel vaulted, the east range contained the chapter room (beside the cloisters), and probably a dayroom to the north side of this; there are fireplaces which presumably served two rooms. Dormitories were overhead.

Location: 6m (10km) east southeast of Ennis on the R469.

BALLINDERRY MIDDLE CHURCH
Ballinderry, County Antrim

One effect of the Protestant Reformation in Ireland was that it transferred a large amount of pre-Reformation ecclesiastical property over to the newly established reformed Church of Ireland. Neither incentive nor opportunity was left to the dispossessed Catholic Church to embark on anything more than small-scale building; in the upshot, many older churches fell into ruin, and many others were destroyed. Indeed, Protestant pastors hardly fared much better: Irish benefices were generally poor, and the population hostile. So there was little church building on either side during the sixteenth-century Tudor period. The last stand and final defeat of old Gaelic Ireland at the Battle of Kinsale in 1602 was followed by the mammoth Plantation of Ulster which threw open half a million acres of Irish land to Protestant settlers from England and Scotland. In 1641, a vicious anti-Protestant backlash was in turn followed by the vengeful massacres of the Cromwellian regime. The Cromwellians were the enemies of Anglicans as well, so that during this regime Church of Ireland clergy were dismissed from their parishes, and Cromwellian preachers installed in their stead. But one of the first acts of Charles II in the Restoration Parliament of 1660 was the re-establishment of the hierarchy of the Established Church. Immediately afterwards, two Church of Ireland archbishops and ten bishops were consecrated together in St Patrick's Cathedral, Dublin.

Among these new appointments the most distinguished was Jeremy Taylor as Bishop of Down, Connor and Dromore. This famous Divine was at this time a close friend of Colonel Arthur Hill of Hillsborough, County Down, where in 1663 he consecrated 'a spacious, well-contrived Church ... dedicated to Saint Malachias' built by Hill. And it was he who, in 1664, close to Hillsborough, built what remains today the best example of a seventeenth-century Church of Ireland parish

Ballinderry Middle Church

church, the Middle Church of Ballinderry, to serve the new Protestant settler community of County Antrim. It is the best example because it retains the essentials of its original appearance, and is thus representative of much that has since disappeared. In form it is just a simple rectangle, its small size partly explained by the presence of a then rival neighbouring Presbyterian church.

This delightful little building is an example of a barn church, a type that occurred mainly in the north of Ireland. The churchyard is entered through a lych-gate which provided a sheltered resting place for the coffin before burial services.

The gallery at the gabled west end is an eighteenth-century addition, reached by a stone stairway built on to the exterior of the church. Large deep rectangular windows on three sides are widely splayed on the inside and filled with oculus panes that admit the light, but are not see-through. There are two small circular windows in the west gable, over which is a simple bell-turret. The communion table and chairs, constructed out of the oak roof timbers of an older ruined church at neighbouring Portmore, are original, as are the oak box-pews with their wooden latches. The baptismal font is also the original; so are the long-handled collecting pans. More recent is the ceiling of oak roof timbers installed in 1902. Of special interest is the triple-decker panelled oak pulpit with its seat for the clerk in the lowest section, its middle section for readings and recital of prayers, and upper section for preaching. And where else can one find another little church like Ballinderry that is still lit by candlelight, with candlesticks attached to the box-pews, pulpit, and reader's desk?

Location: About 8m (13km) west of Lisburn. Open for Church of Ireland Services only.

ST MICHAN'S CHURCH
Dublin, County Dublin

A St Michan's Church was built in 1095 where the present one now stands, its beginnings associated with the Viking founders of Dublin who in that year elected Samuel O'Haingli, a monk of Worcester, as bishop of Dublin. In keeping with Viking tradition, St Michan is said to have been a Danish saint, but he may well have been a Dublin Viking!

For close on 600 years St Michan's was the only parish church on the north side of the River Liffey, served by the Augustinian canons of Christ Church Cathedral, just across the river. At the Reformation it became Church of Ireland. During most of the Restoration years following the return of Charles II in 1660, Ireland was governed for the monarchy by the mighty Duke of Ormond, James Butler, and Dublin began to blossom into a great city. The present St Michan's Church was built in the 1680s to cater to the spiritual needs of a greatly expanded suburban Protestant population, and the design is attributed to the then Surveyor-General, the Yorkshire-born Sir William Robinson (1643-1712), better known as the architect of the great military Royal Hospital at Kilmainham.

St Michan's is one of the earliest galleried churches in Dublin, with a square west end tower, featuring a competent classical west doorway with scrolled pediment, and famous vaults beneath the church. The interior is dignified but simple, and representative of many early eighteenth-century city churches, particularly of those that are no more. A very sumptuous interior version of St Michan's survives at St Werburgh's (1759). Because of its association with the celebrated Baroque composer Handel, the organ here gets more than a usual share of attention – a strong tradition has it that Handel played on this organ during his stay in Dublin at the time of the première performance of his oratorio *Messiah* in 1742. The instrument had been built 18 years earlier by a famous organ builder of Dublin, and is one of the oldest organs still in use in Ireland. It was rebuilt in 1962, but the original three-manual keyboard remains on display at the rear of the church.

A panel in the balcony in front of the organ consists of an incomparably fine carving of 17 musical instruments, wonderfully carved out of one piece of wood. Because of its stylistic similarity to known wood carvings by him, the piece has been attributed to the sculptor John Houghton (+1761) who was associated with the Dublin Society (it became the Royal Dublin Society in 1820), an agency established in 1731 with the objective of 'improving husbandry, manufacture, and the useful arts and sciences'. The work dates from about 1724 when the organ was built, and it is natural to postulate that the carvings of cherubs' heads, flowers and fruit on the organ case are also by Houghton.

The eighteenth-century pulpit was originally mounted on wheels so that it could be moved easily about the church to suit the particular service – or perhaps to wheel out a boring preacher! Also eighteenth-century is the Penitent's Pew, otherwise known as a Stool of Repentance, a movable Prayer Desk that was formerly used as a public confessional: kneeling or standing on this pew, the only one of its type surviving in Dublin, the penitent acknowledged his sins, perhaps reading aloud from the book rest on the back of it.

The baptismal font is also of eighteenth-century vintage. Considering that St Michan's was once a meeting place of the Protestant élite, the water from this font must have flowed on the head of many a well-known personage. One outstanding head was that of the statesman and orator Edmund Burke (1729-97) who, although a Protestant, became an intrepid champion of the oppressed: 'The Protestant Ascendancy is nothing more or less than the resolution of one set of people to consider themselves as the sole citizens of the Commonwealth and to keep a dominion over the rest by reducing them to slavery under a foreign power.'

In 1922 during the Civil War that followed the partitioning of Ireland by the Treaty of 1921, the Four Courts building in Dublin was shelled. Damage to nearby

St Michan's was costly; its original entries of baptism lodged in the public records office were lost, and the fine stained glass window over the sanctuary was shattered by an explosion. The present window was installed in 1958.

It is but a step from the refinements of the church to the dry dust of the vaults below where the temperature remains constant all year round. These long underground passages, with burial chambers ranged along both sides, date from the 1680s when the present church was built. Because of some unique characteristic of the air, the bodies in the vaults have become mummified. Different explanations of this phenomenon have been offered. One is the moisture-absorbing quality of the magnesium limestone from which the vaults are constructed. Another is that the church stands on what was formerly a marshy terrain that supplied to the vaults a high measure of the dry colourless gas methane. In one vault the sides of the wooden coffins have partially fallen away, and the lids have been removed, exposing four of these mummified corpses in a remarkable state of preservation. One is said to have been a nun who lived for over 100 years. The tall central figure is minus his right hand and feet – was he maimed for thievery, or just too tall for his assigned coffin? The figure in the coffin across the back of the chamber is called the Crusader; however, one has difficulty reconciling the relative recency of the vaults with the twelfth or thirteenth-century Crusades. Elsewhere in the vaults the piled-up coffins remain marvellously intact with their velvet coverings and brass nails. The perfidious Lord Leitrim is there in a plain coffin – a man so hated even by his own kin that they never used the vault again!

The Sheares brothers, Henry and John, executed after the Insurrection of 1798, are buried in the vaults of St Michan's. A copy of the execution order is displayed close to the coffins. It was decreed that 'each of them be hanged by the neck, but not until they are dead, for whilst they are yet alive, they are to be taken down, their entrails are to be taken out of their bodies …' and so on through the grisly details of hanging, drawing, and quartering. Some years ago the bodies were re-coffined

Mummified Bodies at St Michan's

after the original coffins were rotted by moisture from flowers brought into the vault.

Location: Church Street. Open daily. Guided tour only.

ST PETER'S CHURCH
Drogheda, County Louth

The defeat of the Catholic cause at the Battle of the Boyne in 1690 ushered in the eighteenth-century Protestant Ascendancy period, during which Catholics were burdened by Penal Laws in a regime of religious persecution exceeding anything the country had ever known. Throughout the century, however, there was a building boom of Protestant churches, particularly in the towns, and in villages adjacent to the estates of the landed gentry. Commencing with St Mary's Church in Dublin, designed by the Surveyor-General, Thomas Burgh (+1730), these churches were predominantly Palladian or classical in architectural design. Standard interiors were rectangular, flat-ceilinged, with galleries on three sides, and a shallow sanctuary at the east end.

St Peter's Church in Drogheda is the finest surviving mid-eighteenth-century Irish provincial town church. It is built on the site of the medieval Collegiate Church of that name. In 1649, as part of a general massacre, Cromwell callously burned down the steeple of this old church to dispose of a terrified group of townspeople who had sought refuge there. Georgian churches of the St Peter's type are no longer common, because many Protestant churches were rebuilt in the nineteenth century.

The design of St Peter's is by the Palladian architect, Hugh Darley (1701-71), with the clock stage of the tower and the spire added by Francis Johnston in 1792 or earlier. Johnston had worked under Thomas Cooley (+1784), deputy state architect and architect to Primate Richard Robinson at Armagh.

The huge central doorcase is set into a semi-circular arch. Two wings flanking the tower have each an architraved window over a pedimented doorway, above which the central tower breaks through the eaves pediment. Deeply cut lunettes pierce the walls at this second stage. At the belfry

St Peter's Church

stage corner pilasters at the angles are set below a Doric entablature; at this stage also there are louvred round-headed openings in the centre, and over each an oculus window surmounted by a pediment resting on console brackets. To this Johnston added a short clock stage (but without the clocks), and the octagonal Gothic needle spire, balustrade, and corner pinnacles.

The main door leads into the large three-bayed classical hall, with the side doors giving access to cantilevered gallery staircases. The U-shaped gallery of rich oak construction is supported by sturdy octagonal piers, and the coved ceiling by unfluted Ionic columns, also of oak. Pointed Y-traceried windows light the nave, short at floor level and tall above the gallery. The four-light stained glass east window in a simple switchline traceried framework is a nineteenth-century insertion. Clear glass had been a popular option during the seventeenth and eighteenth centuries, but colourful stained glass is a pardonable feature of restoration. Heavily moulded cornices add a noble measure of substance and style to the coved ceiling of the nave. An early nineteenth-century painting preserved in the vestry shows the church complete with its box-pews and chandeliers; other than that these have been replaced, Darley's church has been left much as it was. It has its eighteenth-century wrought-iron altar rails, but the communion table with carved Corinthian front is later. At the rear of the church is a fifteenth-century baptismal font showing the Baptism of Christ.

Country houses provided a fruitful outlet for the talents of the great eighteenth-century stuccodores. In the church sphere, however, exuberant Baroque plasterwork ornamentation of the kind found in the Rotunda Hospital Chapel in Dublin is of rare occurrence. How pleasant then to include the highest quality stucco ornamentation, the chief glory of St Peter's. It is concentrated at the east end as an adornment to the sanctuary, and extends to the curved re-entrant corner walls linking the sanctuary and nave. Tall narrow panels framing the east window have eagles on clouds, and open books, and over the window, eagles in curling foliage hold a Bible inscribed with the words 'Holy, holy, holy' in Hebrew; on the side walls are frames with swirling foliage, swags of fruit, cornucopias, and the plumed helmet motif, and below

Stucco Ornamentation in St Peter's

these 32 panels star-studded in gold. The identity of the
stuccodore is unknown, but he was probably of Continental
origin, and his work, notably in that it does not include

Double Cadaver Slab

figures, appears to be influenced by or at least share the characteristics of the Irish plasterwork school that developed after the mid-century, and whose key figure was Ireland's greatest plasterworker, Robert West (+1790).

Outstanding among the memorials mounted on the east end walls is that to the Recorder of Drogheda and later Lord Chief Justice, Henry Singleton (+1780). The Singleton Monument was executed in 1787 by John Hickey (1756-95), sculptor to the Prince of Wales. Hickey was a product of the Dublin Society's Schools. His promising career was cut off in 1795 at the age of 39 – of 'intemperance', it was suggested. Only one other monument by Hickey exists in Ireland, the 1790 monument to David La Touche in Delgany Church, County Dublin. The Singleton Monument displays a bust of the Chief Justice and, appropriately in context, a figure of mourning Justice holding a broken sword and scales. On the opposite side the bust of the commemorated John Ball is set on a sarcophagus.

Among some interesting tombstones in the churchyard is a macabre early sixteenth-century larger than life-size double-cadaver slab intended as a reminder of the awesome reality of human burial and decay. It is the lid of a sarcophagus originally placed inside the medieval Collegiate Church, but now built into the north-east wall of the churchyard. Edward Golding and his wife for whom the tomb was made are shown as skeletons in shrouds tied at the head and feet.

Location: Magdalen Street. Open only for Church of Ireland Services.

ST MALACHY'S CHURCH
Hillsborough, County Down

The primary function of a church is worship. If the church is old and beautiful and sited in picturesque surroundings, the aesthetic effect can also help to raise the soul. St Malachy's Church in the village of Hillsborough shares in all these things. However, its special claim to distinction is as pioneer in the Irish part of the eighteenth-century Gothic Revival in architecture, where it ranks as the finest example of that style.

To bring the architectural scene into perspective – the mid-eighteenth-century Gothic Revival in England, with offshoots in Ireland, constituted a challenge to the staid old classical canon. It came at the very beginning of the Romantic movement in literature, the arts, and philosophy, and was a nostalgic acting out of the medieval world of castles and abbeys. Today it is given the eighteenth-century spelling Gothick to distinguish it from the later Victorian neo-Gothic style. Some patrons of the arts opted for the luxuriance of Gothick in preference to the severity of the classical ideal. A prominent leader of the revival was the English gentleman Sir Horace Walpole (1717-97) who led the way by adding a wealth of Gothick features to his Georgian home at Strawberry Hill near London. Whimsicality and frivolity informed the new mood, translating into an architecture of a lighter sort. Hillsborough Church shares the lightness, but nothing of the triviality of the new mood.

The story of St Malachy's goes back at least to 1662, when Sir Arthur Hill (+1663) began to build a church here on the site of one burned down during the anti-Protestant uprising of 1641. Hill was an artful planter who sagaciously managed to keep the peace with both sides in the war between Charles I and Parliament. Between 1760 and until opened for public worship in 1772, Hill's Church was extensively remodelled and incorporated into the present Church by the then Earl of Hillsborough, Wills Hill (1718-93), Colonial Secretary of State

St Malachy's Church, Hillsborough

under George III. In 1789, Hill became First Marquis of
Downshire. He had hoped that St Malachy's would become
the cathedral church of the diocese of Down – the Bishop's

throne in the south transept is a reminder of this unfulfilled wish. But his was an influential voice in the building of Downpatrick Cathedral, 17 miles southeast of Hillsborough, whose Gothick interior rivals that of St Malachy's.

Reached by a long tree-lined avenue with beautifully tended lawn, the strictly symmetrical St Malachy's is a cruciform building with lofty pinnacled tower and octagonal spire with lucarnes, and square towers at the end of each transept. The nave is aisleless.

The interior decor is tasteful and elegant beyond compare, appearing most prominently in the delicately carved wood furnishings that are mainly of oak. Of particular note is the Cedar of Lebanon panelling of the sanctuary. The highly ornate pulpit, prayer desk, dark oak box-pews, and curved organ-loft are all in the eighteenth-century Gothick style. Unusually high box-pews were common to churches of the period: in an unheated church they provided a modicum of warmth by the exclusion of draughts. Earliest heating attempts date to 1833 when hot air stoves were introduced. The transepts are quite short; elevated above the nave they are reached by short flights of steps. Plush square pews in the transepts are reserved for dignitaries – these are the Downshire and Corporation pews. On display in the north transept is the State Chair from the Chapel Royal in Dublin Castle. It was formerly reserved for the Lord Lieutenant, and is now in Hillsborough with the approval of the Dean and Chapter of Christ Church Cathedral.

The east window by Francis Elginton of Birmingham is to a design by the noted English portrait painter, Sir Joshua Reynolds (1723-92). Restraint is used in the design of the stained glass, and the colour shades of the other windows in the Church have been selected to harmonise with it.

The Snetzler organ in the west gallery was built by order of Wills Hill in 1772, and the bill for the purchase is preserved, along with other effects, in a glass case in the south transept – the cost of the organ was £400. The chamber organ beside the choir is from 1795. Originally in Hillsborough Castle, it was donated to the Church in 1923 by the Marquis of Downshire.

Still on the subject of music, William Harty, father of the noted composer and conductor, Sir Hamilton Harty (1879-1941), was organist of St Malachy's from 1878 to 1918.

Perhaps because of the special air of refinement that permeates this period church, the memorials are particularly apt, the prize going to the Nollekens monument on the north wall of the nave. In those days, only such wealthy patrons as Wills Hill could consider a sculptor of the stature of the eccentric Nollekens (1737-1823) whose monument, to Henry and Peter Leslie, dates from 1774. Joseph Nollekens was born in London, the son of an immigrant Belgian painter; he studied under the eminent sculptor Peter Scheemakers, and became a prolific artist of the first rank.

As late as 1840 it was the custom for the Archdeacon and curate to go to the Castle on special occasions and attend Lord Downshire and his family to church. So little has Hillsborough Church changed that such protocol would hardly seem out of place even today.

Location: Hillsborough. Open daily.

PRIMATE ROBINSON'S CHAPEL
Armagh, County Armagh

Because of its Episcopalian structure, the Church of Ireland accorded its highest ecclesiastical position to the Protestant Archbishop of Armagh, Primate of all Ireland. During the period of the Protestant Ascendancy, the position was one of power and privilege, backed by royal patronage. High on the list of Englishmen who held this office was Richard Robinson (1709-94), who came to Ireland in 1751 as chaplain to the Lord Lieutenant, and in 1765 was nominated to George III for the Archbishopric of Armagh. Robinson then quickly commissioned his chief architect, Thomas Cooley (1740-84), to design some of the finest public buildings that now adorn the city of Armagh, among them an elegant Palace for himself, and a nearby Primate's Chapel. Elsewhere, Cooley is best known as architect of the magnificent Royal Exchange in Dublin, now the City Hall; by the time it was completed in 1779, Cooley had been promoted to deputy state architect.

The Primate's Chapel is numbered among the finest examples of Georgian neo-classical architecture in the country. Construction began in 1781, but Cooley died three years later, and the building was completed in 1786 by the distinguished architect, Francis Johnston (1760-1829), who had earlier worked under Cooley's direction. It is worth noting that the versatile Johnston was competent also in Gothick Revival; by way of example, his design for Ballymakenny Church in County Louth, commissioned by Archbishop Robinson, closely parallels the Gothick style of St Malachy's in Hillsborough.

The exterior of the Primate's Chapel is constructed of ashlar limestone where the close jointing of the stones gives the facing an almost seamless appearance. The tetrastyle Ionic Order portico stands on a platform approached by steps. The choice of Ionic with its slender columns and distinctive capital – the female counterpart of the masculine Doric Order – is

Primate Robinson's Chapel

clearly the appropriate one for this little chapel. Conforming to the norms of strict neo-classical style, thr four pilasters along the face of the building match exactly the four columns

Archbishop's Chair

of the portico. The entablature and pediment are plain except for a series of dentils around the tympanum of the pediment and under the cornice.

The rigid classical symmetry of the exterior continues into

the interior. English oak is used in the wall panelling, pews, and lofty Archbishop's Chair with its classical broken-apex pediment, and the carved joinery is of exceptional quality. The pews set along the side walls on opposite sides of the Chapel were for the servants, and two cushioned and curtained pews in the rear corners were reserved for special guests. Within the framework of an ornamented frieze, rosettes are the main decorative feature in the plaster panels of the coffered ceiling. A cosy musicians' gallery is set into the rear wall at second storey level.

Superlatives expended on a description of this little neo-classical church need not disguise the fact that it was in a less than perfect state when sold to the Armagh District Council in 1975. Restoration work costing £125,000 was undertaken in 1985 and completed in 1986. The superlatives may be reserved for the integrity of a restoration that retained as much as possible of the original. Damaged ceiling panels were replaced and the ceiling repainted in its original shades of delicate blue and yellow. The bulk of the wall panelling remains, sections destroyed by woodworm being replaced. Archbishop Robinson did have a fireplace set into the wall facing his chair, and for the sake of authenticity there is an eighteenth-century fireplace in that position today. Most of the floor tiles are also the originals. New curtains and railings were put on the musicians' gallery and Chapel pews.

Location: Palace Demesne, Friary Street. Open year-round. Guided tour only.

FIRST PRESBYTERIAN CHURCH
Belfast, County Antrim

As part of the Plantation of Ulster which followed the defeat of the last of the old Gaelic chieftains at the Battle of Kinsale in 1602, the counties of Antrim and Down were largely settled with Presbyterians of Scottish origin. Along with their co-religionists in Scotland, the Presbyterians of Ulster opposed the doctrines of the Episcopal Church and the annoying intrusions of the monarchy. In 1698, a beginning of an enduring controversy within the Church itself occurred when the Synod of Ulster required that all licentiates for the ministry be required to subscribe to the 1648 Westminster Confession of Faith, creating a church that is still divided between subscribing and non-subscribing congregations. In 1725, the non-subscribing congregations were placed in a new Presbytery of Antrim, which was given the status of a Synod in the following year. The lot of Presbyterians worsened when, cast in the role of Dissenters, they were barred from public office by a Sacramental Test Act of 1704 – an Act not repealed, and then only partially, until 1780. Their woes were compounded between these dates by the loss through emigration of tens of thousands of Church members.

Until 1708, there was just one congregation of Presbyterians in Belfast. When a second congregation was formed in that year, the original group became the First Congregation and had a T-shaped house of worship on the site of the present Rosemary Street Church that dates from 1783. Since existing Ulster Presbyterian meeting houses are hardly known to predate the mid-eighteenth century, this Rosemary Street Church enjoys the distinction of being among the earliest surviving Presbyterian churches in Ireland.

Built to a design of the leading Belfast architect of his time, Roger Mulholland (1740-1818), who was then ranked as a carpenter, it is elliptical in shape both inside and out, and

Rosemary Street Church

entered by a rectangular hall at the west end. While building was in progress, the illustrious Frederick Hervey, fourth Earl of Bristol and Bishop of Derry – he is mentioned again under St John's Church, Shankill – made a generous donation of 50 guineas towards building costs. Hervey's preference for the oval shape may have weighed with Mulholland, whose design was approved when the problem of roofing a structure of that shape had been solved.

The classical facade of 1783 was modified to its present form in 1833. Anyone viewing a print of the original exterior would agree that some of the old charm has been sacrificed. There have been gains: the present front is the same height but twice the depth of Mulholland's original portico, gains being mainly a more roomy vestibule, two stairways to the gallery, and a Sessions Room at the first floor level. The modified facade has rustication around the windows and entrance doorway, four pairs of Ionic pilasters between three second storey rectangular windows, and a balustrade at roof level. The old brown brick of the oval exterior can be distinguished from the red brick used in most Belfast City buildings from before the mid-nineteenth century.

Any lingering doubts about Rosemary Street Church being Mulholland's best building are immediately dispelled at the sight of the interior. Walk to the north end of the Church, and turn around to admire the magnificent sweep of the curved panelled gallery frontage supported by slender Corinthian columns, the incurve of the short bow, ornamented with carved wreaths, that joins the side galleries, and the curves of the ground floor aisles that match and complement those of the overhanging galleries.

Restoration work completed in 1976 revealed the beauty of the old oak box-pews. For a church to have retained its old box-pews at all is to give it a special distinction. But in the seventeenth and eighteenth centuries box-pews were the norm, and it was customary for individuals and families to lease and sub-let specially allocated pews, treating them much as private property that they personally soft-furnished and maintained. Certainly they were a symbol of class distinction, and nobody at will went through the latched wooden door of an assigned pew with its surround of high panelling providing a measure of privacy and protection from cold draughts. In Rosemary Street the original seating plan provided a continuous oval aisle parallel to the church walls, but in 1872 pews were installed at the southern end of the ellipse, thus creating two separate curving aisles – at the worst, a minor modification of a grand old setting. In the perspective of near-enough history, it is of sad revealing interest to observe that the nineteenth-century ecclesiologists of the neo-Gothic revival called for an end to the auditory church with its marvellous three-decker pulpit and wonderful box-pews.

The pulpit was a gift to the new Meeting House. Six years later there was an historic moment when John Wesley (1703-91), English evangelist and founder of Methodism, preached from this pulpit. It appears, however, that in the crowded conditions of this grand moment a measure of thieving occurred, and a second visit was refused! The north end was extended in 1906, before which the pulpit stood against the unbroken curve of the north wall. On the fiftieth anniversary of the ordination of the Reverend William Bruce in 1862, a stained glass Venetian window was installed behind the pulpit. At the same time the sounding-board of the pulpit – that canopy or tester over the pulpit which served as an acoustical device to project the preacher's voice – was removed and used as a communion table. It is now preserved in the Sessions Room. Since 1906 the pulpit has been backed by the organ console that breaks the full ellipse of the walls and blocks the view of the north window. It is arguable that the organ was better placed in the bow of the gallery where it had stood since 1853.

First House is a particularly brightly lit church thanks to the deep, round-headed, ground glass windows installed in 1873 and ranged along both sides of the gallery walls. The wall spaces between the windows taper up to merge gracefully into the lightly decorated plaster radial ceiling. During the civil disturbances of the 1970s the Church was shaken by nearby car bombs. The ceiling was damaged beyond recovery and was completely replaced. The large centre section of the Bruce window was also destroyed but the original smaller side windows remain.

In 1975, this Church, described by John Wesley as beautiful in the highest degree and the completest place of worship he had ever seen, was listed as part of Ulster's Architectural Heritage as the oldest church in Belfast, and it remains a handsome edifice of great architectural and historic interest.

Location: Rosemary Street. Open for Sunday Services and on Wednesday mornings.

CHURCH OF ST JOHN THE EVANGELIST
Coolbanagher, County Laois

The Church of St John the Evangelist at Coolbanagher deserves special notice as the only one designed by the great London-born architect, James Gandon, who had been apprenticed to the illustrious neo-classicist Sir William Chambers, and settled in Dublin in 1781, where he designed some of the city's finest public buildings. Gandon had come to Ireland under the patronage of John Dawson, later first Earl of Portarlington, and was engaged to design the neo-classical mansion known as Emo Court – and a nearby parish church for Coolbanagher. The church was completed in 1786, and replaced an earlier one whose thatched roof had been set on fire in 1779 during a Sunday Service.

The exterior of the church is strikingly plain and unadorned, and the darkening of the rendering has imparted to it a rather dull appearance. There is a west-end tower with the later addition of an octagonal spire.

A picture hanging in the vestibule attributed to James Malton (1761-1803) shows the church interior as it was originally. The view is of the nave as seen from the sanctuary end. Gandon is standing in the foreground, in conversation with the well-attired John Dawson and a clergyman. Recent restoration departed from the perfect blueprint supplied by this picture, the main difference being in the dark openwork timber ceiling that replaced Gandon's barrel-vault. In the Malton picture the arc of the vault is divided into three compartments. The coffered bands separating these compartments are of equal width and continue down the side walls of the nave in line with the broad floor-to-ceiling pilasters set between the windows on each side. By cutting off the ceiling bands the former spaciousness conveyed by the unified design of walls and ceiling was lost but the side walls remain just as they were, and the genuine classical touch is secured by a discreet use of festoons and swags, and the

Interior of Coolbanagher Church

plaster classical urns set into deep round-headed niches.

Triumphal arches being among Gandon's favourite themes, each side wall is a blank arcade simulating a row of three triumphal arches. The triumphal arch of Imperial Rome provided the model for many later classical imitations. In the model, the majestic semi-circular central arch through which victorious legions passed is flanked by columns or pilasters which support an entablature below an upper 'attic' storey. On each side of the central arch there is either a smaller passage or spacious wall niche. In the Gandon simulation the central arch of each triumphal arch is suggested by the high semi-circular church window, and the side walls by flat pilasters and deep round-headed niches containing large classical urns. Altogether an engaging and imaginative effect.

Again looking at the Malton picture, one can regret that the old box-pews have been replaced by conventional seating, the usual arrangement when it has been decided to change seating; perhaps because of custom, today's churchgoers feel more at ease in open pews. One also notices that the bow front of the little gallery above the vestibule has been removed.

The twelfth-century baptismal font now preserved in the nave was recovered from the Pleasure Grounds of Emo Park, where it may well have done service as a bird bath, a flower planter, or a piece of ornamental sculpture.

Location: About 5m (8km) south of Portarlington. Open daily.

ST MARY'S PRO-CATHEDRAL
Dublin, County Dublin

Throughout the latter half of the eighteenth century, English architects were largely preoccupied with the neo-classical movement and the rediscovery of the authentic buildings of ancient Greece. Beginning with James Stuart's Doric Temple of Theseus at Ragley, Worcestershire, in 1758, Greek temples became the vogue and, for almost a century, the Greek Doric and Ionic Orders were applied to a wide spectrum of buildings, including churches. From about 1770, the course of architecture in Ireland was largely charted by English architects – Wyatt, Cooley, Gandon, and others – some of whom resided in Ireland. In the light of all this it is ironic that Catholic Ireland's mightiest Greek Revival church, the Pro-Cathedral in Dublin, should have been designed by an amateur Dublin architect named John Sweetman.

But was it? Some say it was not Sweetman but a French architect, Louis Hippolyte le Bas, and others that it was Sweetman using the design of a Paris church by le Bas. At this time (1814), Sweetman was living in Paris, having already been imprisoned in Scotland for his part in the Irish insurrection of 1798. In either event, discretion was called for – Catholic Emancipation was not yet a reality – so the plan came marked with only the letter P – P for Paris? And, whether really called for or not, discretion was also used in the siting of the building. Instead of its being located in the then available prestigious main street position now occupied by the General Post Office, it was tucked down a side street where its cramped position allows only a close-up view of two sides of the building.

It was, nonetheless, the fulfilment of the dream of Archbishop John Thomas Troy (1786-1823), his professed dream of a dignified and spacious church to replace his old mensal parish church in Liffey Street. St Mary's Metropolitan Chapel, as it was called at its dedication in 1825 – the title Pro-

Cathedral did not come until the 1880s – is a massive Greek Revival building. Following the example of Stuart, the entrance portico, with its hexastyle fluted Doric columns of Portland stone, is in imitation of the Theseum in Athens. Economy and severity, and more emphatically, strength, are the keynotes of the mighty Doric Order with its huge tapering columns carrying an entablature complete with triglyphs, metopes, mutules and guttae, over which rises a plain pediment with statuary at the angles.

The exterior is Greek Revival at its best, but in odd contrast the interior includes many of the characteristics of a basilica – the main basilical ingredients being the apse, the barrel vaulted nave ceiling higher than those of the aisles, and the 22 fluted Doric columns that form a great colonnade between nave and aisles and around the curve of the apse, and the crypt under the church at the sanctuary end. Apart from the crypt, the Roman basilica provided the model for that type of Christian church still known as a basilica. The aisled nave also begins here, its wider central section being then reserved for men. Exactly matching that of the exterior is the entablature above the central section of the nave. Regrettably, the representations of saints' heads that formerly adorned the metopes of the frieze have been painted over.

An arresting facet of the architecture of St Mary's is the coffered dome that rises above three giant lunettes, the two side ones providing the main church lighting. However, an original well-preserved model of the Cathedral shows no dome, and when the dome was added it was not received without plenty of demur. Undoubtedly the earliest Christian basilicas did not have domes; these were a later adaptation from Byzantine architecture. Purists may have difficulty reconciling a dome with the sharp exterior lines of a Grecian temple.

The interior embellishment has benefited by contributions from the hands of three early nineteenth-century sculptors of exceptional merit – Turnerelli, Smyth, and Hogan. Peter Turnerelli (1774-1839) was Belfast-born of Italian parents; his high altar table with carvings of adoring

Interior of St Mary's

tabernacle has been set to the rear. Also by Turnerelli is the
nave aisle monument to John Troy with the recumbent effigy

of an archbishop. In both cases, Turnerelli's carving shows an awareness of fifteenth-century Italian sculpture style. The artistic plaster relief of the Ascension of Christ framed by the lunette above the altar is the work of the neo-classical sculptor John Smyth (1773-1840), one time Head of the Sculpture School of the Dublin Society. Biblical scenes against a gold background are set into the pendentives on each side of the relief. John Hogan (1800-58), son of a Cork builder and educated in Cork and Rome, had a special predilection for classical themes, but his output also included religious subjects commissioned for Ireland. The elaborate funerary memorial to Peter Purcell, founder of the Agricultural Society of Ireland, is a good example of Hogan's work – now on the wall of the church office, a walled-off corner of the nave.

Archbishop Troy was succeeded by Dr Daniel Murray (1823-52), who is commemorated by a huge marble monument in the north aisle executed by Sir Thomas Farrell (1827-1900). This memorial is matched in the south aisle by an even more elaborate monument, also by Farrell, to Dr Murray's successor, Dr Paul Cullen (1852-78). Early in his episcopate, Dr Cullen was active in promoting a Catholic University for Dublin, and in 1854 presided at the installation of John Henry Newman as its first Rector. Scenes encircling the base of the Cullen monument are symbolic of his active interests – care for the poor, training of priests, and education.

After the death of Archbishop Cullen, St Mary's Metropolitan Chapel began to be called the Pro-Cathedral, and the continued lack of a proper cathedral church in the predominantly Catholic diocese of Dublin remains as something of an anomaly. Nothing, however, can substitute for the part that the Pro-Cathedral has played in the political and religious life of Ireland. It was the scene of the lying-in-state in 1847 of the champion of Catholic Emancipation, Daniel O'Connell, the Liberator; of the Republican leader Michael Collins in 1922, and of Ireland's President Eamon De Valera in 1975. It was at the heart of the centenary of Catholic Emancipation celebrations in 1928, and of the Eucharistic Congress in 1932. It has had a good life, and the recent restoration has given it the promise of many more years.

Worthy of mention here because of its stylistic similarity to the Pro-Cathedral is the splendid late Classical Revival Dominican church on Pope's Quay in Cork, begun in 1832, and set off by an impressive hexastyle Ionic portico with fluted columns.

Location: Marlborough Street. Open daily.

ST JOHN'S CHURCH
Shankill, County Kilkenny

The Board of First Fruits, established in 1711, was a Church of Ireland body authorised to use the accumulated First Fruits (the first year's revenue, or annates, of each benefice) to buy back impropriate tithes (tithes paid to laymen who had come into possession of Church properties and lands after the suppression of the monasteries by Henry VIII) and, within certain restraints, to use this revenue to build and repair churches and glebe houses. Until the coffers of the Board were supplemented by sizeable annual Parliamentary grants commencing in 1777, the Board's operation remained sluggish. Between 1791 and 1803 it granted a standard sum of £500 each for the building of some 90 churches, along with a grant of £100 towards the purchase of each of about 120 glebe houses. A Parliamentary Act of 1808 gave the Board a free hand and increased grants which peaked to a sizeable £60,000 in the year 1816, and tapered off to £10,000 in 1823, after which the grants ceased. By 1832 there were close to 1,300 Church of Ireland churches of which about 1,200 were of parish church type, and of these about 700 owed their existence in whole or in part to funding by the Board of First Fruits.

Most of the surviving country Church of Ireland parish churches date from the period 1810-30, and St John's Church in Shankill has been selected here simply because it is typical of the hundreds of churches built to the almost standard plan that it exemplifies. Any one of a hundred others would have done quite as well. Many of these are being gradually abandoned and are beginning to fall into ruin and, because of dwindling attendance, only sparing use is made of most. St John's illustrates the basic theme, and if it is patterned to any architectural style, it must be called Gothic. There is a small plain gabled hall with a square tower built on to the west end. Walls are of rubble stone and rendered in lime plaster. The

St John's Church, Shankill

tower has corner pinnacles and a semblance of battlements, and on each upper face a louvred window with a pointed arch and hood moulding. Below this recessed blank panels further help to break the monotony of the walls. Windows along the north and south walls are pointed and have simple Y-tracery.

The model for the typical Board of First Fruits churches of the 1810-30 building boom goes back to the 1770s when Frederick Hervey, fourth Earl of Bristol and Bishop of Derry, was making a name for himself as a builder of fine houses and churches. Some churches of Hervey's earlier building phase – for example, Tyanee Church, County Derry (near Portglenone, County Antrim) – would double for St John's and scores of others of its type.

There are variations on the basic theme; they may be merely cosmetic, like the presence of a clock on the tower wall, more elaborate window tracery, or a shallow sanctuary at the east end. Or they may be considerable, like the addition of an elegant spire, or a transept. Occasionally, the services of an architect of distinction made the difference, but usually it merely added up to money – a loan accompanying the Board of First Fruits grant, an influential patron, or additional money from other sources. What better instances of this than the uncommonly well-dressed First Fruits parish churches of Buttevant (1826) and Carrigaline (1828), both in County Cork and both designed by the noted English immigrant brothers James and George Richard Pain who worked extensively in Munster?

Location: On N9 at Shankill near Paulstown.

ST PATRICK'S CATHEDRAL
Armagh, County Armagh

Since the time of St Patrick, the City of Armagh has been the primatial see of the Catholic Church and, since the Reformation, of the Church of Ireland, the Protestant Cathedral standing on the site given to Patrick by the chieftain Daire. In spite of repeated burnings and plunderings, a cathedral always stood on this ancient site, the present Church of Ireland building being an enlarged version of a rebuilding of the 1260s. It was not until the Catholic Emancipation Act of 1829 was passed that the Catholic archbishop returned to residence in Armagh after a three centuries-long absence.

The foundation stone of the Catholic Cathedral, to be built to a Perpendicular Gothic plan of Thomas Duff of Newry, was laid in 1840 by Archbishop William Crolly (1835-49). A drawing of the original plan shows an edifice with a square central tower, two smaller square towers on the west side, and a mass of frilly-looking pinnacles set around the towers and along the walls. As planned, the building had hardly risen to 20 feet when construction was halted by the Great Famine, and when building was resumed in 1854, both architect and archbishop were dead. James Joseph McCarthy (1817-82), the Irish 'Pugin', who succeeded Duff, then radically changed the design from Perpendicular (as seen in Duff's Newry cathedral) to Decorated Gothic; that is, from a fifteenth/sixteenth-century to a fourteenth-century style. In Roman days it might have been interpreted as a bad omen, but it appears that an open-air Mass to celebrate the post-famine resumption of work at Armagh was mercilessly lashed by a torrential storm of hail, rain, and wind. A more auspicious event was a fund-raising bazaar of 1865 that brought in £7,000, and for which prizes were contributed from Rome and France – including a grandfather clock which still stands unclaimed in the vestry! The exterior was finished by 1873 during the episcopate of Archbishop David McGettigan

(1870-89), and the interior in 1904 during that of his successor, Michael Logue.

As though to emphasise its status as primatial cathedral of the Catholic Church in Ireland, the twin-spired Cathedral Church of St Patrick stands on an eminence reached by way of a seven-terraced set of steps. The switch to fourteenth-century Decorated Gothic removed all the fussiness from its outward appearance and, if allowance is made for the disproportionate shortness of the spires set on what were originally planned as square west-front towers, the Cathedral presents a dignified and imposing face. Interesting remnants of the Perpendicular style are the wide west doorways with pointed arches under a square arrangement of the door mouldings.

In the interior, only the merest impression can be conveyed of the exotic decorative detail that covers the walls of the nave from floor to ceiling in mosaics consisting of small variously-coloured fragments of pottery and glass, an excellently durable material for coping with the damp Irish climate. The spandrels over the nave arcade are ornamented with colourful medallions of the patron saints of 20 Irish dioceses, which stand out in colour against a gold background. Some are well known like Saints Patrick and Brigid, others less well known like Saints Eden and Asicus. At the clerestory level carved angels hold shields showing the arms of the dioceses of Ireland. Every bit of wall space around and between the medallions and shields is filled with scrolls and swirling curves and trumpeting winged angels. The crowning mosaic is that above the arch of the crossing facing the nave; St Patrick is here depicted baptising and converting the Irish. The intensity of the ornamentation and figure representation in the nave continues undiminished throughout the crossing and transepts.

Oil paintings depicting 24 incidents in the lives of famous Irish saints are set along the ceiling: Ireland's three patron saints are there, along with Malachy, and Brendan, and Laurence O'Toole. The paintings are the work of the Italian artist, Oreste Amici, executed in a prevailing tone of subdued terracotta that blends with the colour of the wall mosaics.

Most of the stained glass windows came from Munich, but that of the Lady Chapel came from Dublin as a gift from Archbishop McGettigan. Biblical scenes are everywhere portrayed in glowing colours.

Vatican II prescriptions led to major alterations in the arrangement of the sanctuary. For the 60 years following 1904 a magnificent high altar of Italian marble stood at the east end of the crossing framed by a highly decorated five-arched rood screen. The archbishop's throne was also of marble, and the massive pulpit to a design of Medici of Florence stood on a base of Italian marble. All these rich furnishings have been replaced by contemporary furnishings designed by Liam McCormick and Partners of Derry. The aim of opening up the sanctuary has been achieved, but the result is certain to call forth mixed reactions. Wicklow granite was used in the shaping of the new altar, ambo, and tabernacle stand. The only part of the old arrangement considered worthy of retention was the Caen stone reredos of what was formerly the Lady Chapel which occupied the space between the high altar and the east wall of the church. Together with the great stained glass east window it now forms a magnificent backdrop to the open sanctuary area.

Since the time of Dr Paul Cullen, Ireland's first resident Cardinal, successive Archbishops of Armagh have also been received into the College of Cardinals. In an historical feature special to Armagh Cathedral and a gesture symbolising passing human glory, the hats of deceased cardinals hang untended from the ceiling of the aisle close to the Lady Chapel.

St Patrick's is just one of four cathedrals – the others are at Monaghan, Derry, and Thurles – and some 40 other churches built by J.J. McCarthy, the leading Catholic ecclesiologist after Pugin. His Lombardo-Romanesque cathedral at Thurles, County Tipperary, is a rare departure from his dedication to neo-Gothicism.

Location: Cathedral Road. Open daily.

ST MALACHY'S CHURCH
Belfast, County Antrim

Throughout the nineteenth century Belfast developed into a modern, highly-industrialised city and thousands flocked there in search of jobs, including large numbers of Catholics whose resident numbers increased from a little more than 1,000 in 1800 to about 30,000 in 1840. There was a manifest need for new churches. Providentially, it must have seemed, the handsome sum of £3,000 was bequeathed by one Captain Thomas Griffith of Belfast for the erection of a Catholic Church, and it supplied the means for what was to become the finest late-Georgian Tudor Revival building in the city.

Tudor architecture proper flourished throughout the sixteenth century, being preceded by and sharing some of the characteristics of Perpendicular Gothic – the mass of vertical lines, the flattened four-centred arch, and the fan vault.

The foundation stone of the T-shaped St Malachy's Church was laid in 1841 and the building was dedicated in 1844. The architect was Thomas Jackson (1807-90), a native of Waterford, who practiced in Belfast and was once a partner of Thomas Duff, the designer of Newry Cathedral. Like Duff, Jackson worked in both classical and Tudor styles, but he was more at ease in Tudor Revival, an aspect of his designing skills to which St Malachy's bears ample testimony.

The sixteenth-century Tudor fashion for brick appears in the exterior walls. Tall, octagonal, battlemented turrets frame the central gable, with matching shorter turrets at the sides, and a central turret from which the spire has been removed. Parapets run right along the walls and gables like a string-course. All is in the manner of Hampton Court Palace, London (1514), built by the Tudor King Henry VIII. Flattened arches and horizontal bars at mid-height put the Tudor stamp on all the windows; absent, however, is the common feature of a horizontal hood-moulding with enclosed spandrels immediately above the arches, and the panel tracery to be

St Malachy's Church, Belfast

expected in the Perpendicular context is non-existent. At once strange and imposing, the exterior gives just a little hint of the extraordinarily splendid interior of this church. The suspended frothy fan-vaulted ceiling immediately arrests the eye; it in turn is recognisably similar to but a scaled-down version of the ceiling of Tudor King Henry VII Chapel in Westminster Abbey. An essential feature of the fan-vault is the inverted cone with concave sides, the addition of the pendent giving it a shuttlecock look. The cones in St Malachy's are in rows along the ceiling, with half cones beside the walls, and the spaces between the rows are filled with spoked circles. Pugin would have had his reservations about the lavish display of plaster work, but the effect remains stunning.

In a departure from normal Catholic practice, the high altar and two side altars are positioned along one of the longer sides of the church. This was to meet the requirement that a maximum amount of gallery space be provided, which Jackson did by placing a long, wide gallery along the wall

Interior of St Malachy's

facing the altar and extending along the two shorter sides. This ample gallery is six seats in depth – more than enough for the congregation of the 1850s – and suggests that St

Malachy's may have been intended as a cathedral for the diocese, a suspicion reinforced by the fact that one bishop was actually consecrated here in 1860.

The wall behind the present post-Vatican II altar table was formerly the reredos of the elaborately ornamented high altar dedicated in 1926. The altar piece was crafted by a member of a refugee family from Italy named Piccioni. This old altar has been moved back against the sacristy wall, where it now combines with the former reredos to create a magnificent backdrop to the present altar arrangement. With its Tudor arches springing from slim banded columns, its drop-tracery, quatrefoils and other lacy decoration, the reredos rises resplendent to the ceiling. The old marble pulpit has been left untouched beside the altar.

During air-raid attacks on Belfast in 1941, St Malachy's Church narrowly escaped total destruction when a bomb struck a nearby distillery. Windows were blown out and stained glass shattered. New windows across the front of the Church reproduce the old design, but with artificial stone frames instead of wood. The eight-light window over the main entrance was renewed with complicated fan tracery in the decorated Tudor style. Damage to the ceiling by flying debris was fortunately limited to two panels, enabling the ceiling to be restored to its former condition.

Visitors to the ancient monastic ruins at Mellifont and Monasterboice in County Louth can supplement the Tudor Revival experience of St Malachy's by continuing on to Collon Parish Church, where the model for the interior was the Chapel of King's College, Cambridge, with the slim clustered shafts of each bay supporting a frail-looking plaster fan-vault. Funding for Collon church included a substantial grant and loan from the Board of First Fruits, making possible a luxury far beyond the average standard of Board churches.

Location: Alfred Street. Open daily.

ST MARY'S CATHEDRAL
Killarney, County Kerry

In the great English architect Augustus Welby Pugin (1812-52) one encounters a genius whose architectural credo is as interesting – well, almost so – as his actual body of church designs. A convert to Catholicism in 1833, Pugin became a fiery and outspoken exponent of Gothic revivalism. 'All I have to implore you is to study the subject of ecclesiastical architecture with true Catholic feeling. Do not consider the restoration of ancient art as a mere matter of taste, but remember that it is most closely connected with the revival of the faith itself. ...' Pugin's philosophy was that classical architecture mirrored the material and profane, while a revival of Gothic signalled a return to the ideals of medieval Christianity.

Commissions in Ireland, particularly in County Wexford, formed an important part of Pugin's practice. His best Irish church is St Mary's Cathedral, Killarney – the recognisably similar St Aidan's Cathedral, Enniscorthy, County Wexford, is a close second. Building was begun in 1842, the work being conducted by the Wexford builder Richard Pierce in whom Pugin placed much trust. Suddenly Ireland was devastated by the Great Famine produced by the failure of the potato crop from 1845 to 1847. The unfinished church was boarded up and construction was not resumed until 1853. Work after that date was under the direction of James Joseph MacCarthy, the 'Irish Pugin', disciple and successor of Pugin who had died of a stroke in 1852. The Cathedral was consecrated in 1855. Later construction dating to the first decade of this century included the addition of the spire to the bell-tower, work completed by the firm of Ashlin and Coleman. It adds a measure of ornamentation that Pugin would probably not have endorsed. George Ashlin (1837-1921) trained and worked with Pugin's son, Edward. Their finest achievement in church building was Cobh Cathedral, County Cork, begun

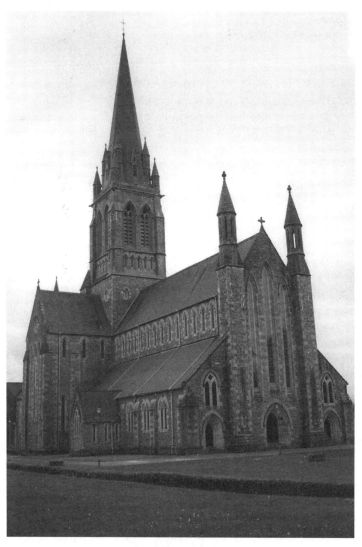

Killarney Cathedral

in 1868 but not completed until the second decade of this century. Ashlin's Killarney spire, with its elegant spirelets and lucarnes around the base, soars to almost 300feet (90m). It was completed in 1912, at which time also the nave was extended from five bays to seven.

Pugin shared the Cistercian attitude that it was appropriate to Catholic principles and the dignity of religion to curtail unnecessary ornament. The ideal Irish cathedral might well be a Cistercian abbey church adapted to cathedral needs, and it may still be possible to see Killarney Cathedral as such a church. The exterior is lofty and impressive but hardly overwhelming. It has the two-storey Cistercian elevation with a row of smallish clerestory windows – no attempt at ostentatious mid-storey walkways. There is a certain severity, with little ornamentation beyond the stone dressings at the angles of the buttresses, and the simple hood mouldings over the windows.

A verdict on the interior may be more challenging. During the 1970s, Killarney Cathedral was faced with the twin tasks of needed interior repair, and the usual sanctuary alterations demanded by Vatican II. In response to the first, the smooth white plasterwork was stripped from the walls, exposing the bare rubble stonework. A genuine medieval touch was definitely lost here. But nothing that has happened detracts from the severity of Pugin's nave arcade with its lightly chamfered pointed arches springing from the discreetly moulded rings and hollows of octagonal capitals and abaci over plain circular columns. And the unadorned vault of the nave has been retained. In the upshot, and counting the tall slim triplets of well-separated lancet windows in the east and west walls, the stamp of Early English Gothic remains reasonably well impressed on the architecture of Killarney Cathedral.

In fulfilment of the requirements of the new liturgy the altar was brought forward from the chancel into the crossing, where it stands beautifully framed by the four great pillars supporting the tower and spire. The accompanying furnishings are the bishop's and celebrant's chairs made of Tasmanian oak, and the lectern placed on a limestone column. The old Victorian high altar and choir stalls have been removed, and, except for the centrally-placed Shrine of the

Blessed Sacrament, designed by Heinz Gernot of Cologne, the area east of the crossing now stands empty. It is a radical transformation, and one wonders what Pugin would think of his 'medieval' cathedral today.

The old arrangement of the chancel – with its high altar set off against the beautiful reredos designed by Pugin's son, Edward, in 1854, and flanked by the rows of choir stalls backed by screens set between the chancel arches – this at least could have been left intact as a museum of Victoriana, without impeding in any way the present one. In Pugin's view, ecclesiastical decoration concentrated especially on the altar and chancel was to be the *first* consideration in a Catholic church. Would it not then have been a feasible compromise to preserve at least the spirit of Pugin in the guise of the old chancel area?

The former Blessed Sacrament Chapel off the north transept was not affected by the renovation, and although it was not completed until 1858, six years after his death, it fully reflects the spirit of Pugin. Of especial note are the sculptured Old Testament scenes in the reredos, each a biblical reference to the Eucharist. Something of Pugin's design also remains in the Kenmare Chantry Chapel off the south transept; the Earls of Kenmare were wealthy patrons of the Cathedral since its beginning, and their family vault is under the chapel. Here again the arresting feature is the magnificent reredos decorated with scenes from the life of the Blessed Virgin.

Killarney Cathedral had a special place in the mind and heart of Pugin. In the words of his son, Edward: 'He tried to make it a splendid temple to Almighty God and at the same time ... suited to the beauty and majesty (with) which the God of Heaven had clothed every hill and valley of that earthly paradise.'

To conclude: it has been said that Pugin's buildings are Pugin and not medieval Gothic. It has also been claimed that Pugin's Irish churches are the best he produced. In the light of these two assertions, the Pugin experience only begins in Killarney. It is not complete without visits to some of his Wexford churches, with preliminary preparation in the form of visits to the ruined St Brendan's Cathedral at Ardfert in County Kerry, and the Cistercian Dunbrody Abbey in County Wexford, from both of which Pugin drew inspiration for his Irish designs. Gorey, Tagoat, and Barntown are the places to see. It hardly matters that St Michael's, Gorey, has a Romanesque mien and lacks the planned spire; like the others, the fine Italian hand of the Master is there for all to see.

Location: Cathedral Place. Open daily.

FIRST PRESBYTERIAN CHURCH
Banbridge, County Down

There was a moment late in the eighteenth century when, through the impact of the American War of Independence and the French Revolution, strong support existed among Presbyterians for the movement of the United Irishmen that sought to make Ireland a republic free of English rule. The resulting nationalist uprising of 1798 was, of course, a failure, and in 1800 the Act of Union brought into being the United Kingdom of Great Britain and Ireland. For their support of the Union, the Presbyterians were rewarded by significant increases in the Royal Grant, the source of salaries paid to ministers, and with the foundation in 1840 of the General Assembly of the Presbyterian Church in Ireland, the Presbyterians of Ulster had reached a high point of strength and solidarity.

Banbridge First Presbyterian Church in Downshire Street dates from 1846 and comes at the end of the Presbyterian preoccupation with Greek Revival which marked the new prosperity, expressed in a move towards the provision of bigger and better Meeting Houses. The severity and sturdiness of the Greek Orders made their appeal, perhaps unconsciously, to those same stern qualities in the Presbyterian character and outlook. In 1828, the First Presbyterian Congregation of Derry had enhanced their old eighteenth-century Meeting House by the addition of a temple-front. Three years later the Belfast Third Congregation in Rosemary Street built a church set off with an impressive tetrastyle portico of cast iron Doric columns. Large Doric columns in a recessed portico were also featured in the First Presbyterian Church in Antrim town, begun in 1834. These and other improvements indicated that the Presbyterian picture had come a long way from the modest small rectangular houses of the previous century.

Not all the nineteenth-century Meeting Houses have

survived but an enduring and beautiful example is found in the Banbridge First Presbyterian Church. The congregation who built this Church was non-subscribing – that is, it was numbered among the Presbyterians of Banbridge who, as far back as the 1720s, had refused to subscribe to the Westminster Confession of Faith. At the opening of the church the guest speaker was no less a person than the illustrious Dr Henry Montgomery, the leading early nineteenth-century spokesman for non-subscription. In contrast to the strident tones of Dr Henry Cooke, Moderator of the Synod of Ulster, his was the voice of moderation on the thorny issues of subscription and Catholic Emancipation.

The Church is a particularly handsome edifice with an attractive pedimented prostyle portico in the Greek Ionic style – there are four fluted freestone columns supporting an elegantly plain entablature and pediment, where grandeur is restrained by the need for propriety. The relative lightness and grace of the Ionic Order gives the right proportion of strength to the building. At the second storey level of the facade are five blank framed panels between tall pilasters, and at first storey level deep wall niches with rounded arches flanking the entrance doorway.

The nave is entered through a spacious flagged vestibule with curving staircases at each side leading up to the U-shaped gallery supported by delicate cast-iron Ionic columns. It is brightly lighted by large clear-glass sash windows above and below the gallery level. The old box-pews survive, and many are even upholstered. Two curved staircases with wrought-iron balusters lead up to the panelled pulpit set in a high position between the galleries, its lower section occupied by the reader's desk. The wall behind the pulpit is covered from pulpit top to ceiling by a huge square panel of green marble with flanking pilasters and Ionic fluted columns. Here is the perfect stage for the preaching function central to Presbyterian worship – striking and dignified, but always (like the exterior) held within the limits of propriety. The coved ceiling suffered bomb damage during the troubles in Northern Ireland, but has been redecorated: there are large

First Presbyterian Church, Banbridge

heavily-moulded rectangular panels and a circular centrepiece in a delicate two-colour scheme. In a particularly imaginative touch, the panels in the soffits under the outer edges of the galleries are decorated in a matching colour design.

From about 1850, and influenced by architects like W.J. Barre (1830-67), a native of Newry and pupil of Thomas Duff, Ulster Presbyterian church building style began to dispense with temple-fronts and veer towards Gothic, but not to the exclusion of many eccentric elements.

Location: Downshire Street. Open only for Sunday Services.

ST FIN BARRE'S CATHEDRAL
Cork, County Cork

'I was brought up in the thirteenth-century belief, and in that belief I intend to die.' It was this faith of the London architect, William Burges (1827-81), which produced the Cathedral Church of St Fin Barre in Cork, the most splendid among the some 30 cathedrals of the Church of Ireland.

Between 1693 and 1738, during a period of rapid city growth, the affluent Protestants of Cork built all of six churches, including St Ann's, Shandon, with its famous bells, and a cathedral of St Fin Barre which was demolished in 1865. An international competition for a new cathedral required a ceiling of £15,000 for the design, with seating for 700. Out of close to 70 entries William Burges won the competition. There was an outcry when it became evident that the Burges design would cost much more than the ceiling figure – in the end it cost more than seven times that figure! – and that the capacity pew space was well shy of the required seating figure. Burges weathered the storm and the main part of the Cathedral was consecrated in 1870, the three towers and spires being completed in 1879. The Burges saga as such is not the abiding irony of St Fin Barre's, but the fact that the Church of Ireland embarked on such an elaborate building exercise on the eve of its disestablishment.

Because of a natural urge to see what is inside, it all too frequently happens that the exterior of a church building receives scant recognition. This can hardly happen at St Fin Barre's, where the eye is completely captivated by the beauty and diversity of the architectural details with their decided preference for thirteenth-century Gothic, and a fair bias in favour of the French form of the same. Viewed from any angle the effect is spectacular. On the west front are the three deeply recessed arched doorways under triangular gables; over these the rose window depicting the Creation, and the twin towers with their octagonal spires and pinnacles;

St Fin Barre's Cathedral

behind these the central tower and spire soaring upwards to a height of 240feet (73m). On the east side is the semi-circular bulk of the apse set against the central tower and transepts.

The west front doorways are a study in themselves. The statuary in the north and south portals represents the Apostles, the four Evangelists, and John the Baptist; the central portal has the figures of the five wise and five foolish virgins of Jesus' parable, with the bridegroom in the centre. Significant Biblical scenes are depicted in the tympana over the three portals, and the soffits of the arches are carved with representations of various trades and professions. In all of this the medieval custom of using human forms as the main embellishment of portals is followed. Animal figures are reserved for the gargoyles (a thirteenth-century innovation) above the portals, with prominently projecting allegorical figures depicting the contest between virtues and vices, the virtue in each case being represented by a woman.

Emblems of the four Evangelists are carved in the spandrels surrounding the rose window, and the uncomplicated tracery of the window itself indicates that the elaborations of fourteenth-century Decorated Gothic are altogether absent from St Fin Barre's, where the window forms are quite simple throughout.

This leaves the decoration of the two-stage towers, the upper level featuring corner pinnacles, each one made up of a spirelet set on a two-tiered circle of short round shafts with capitals (an Early English arrangement), with an arcade of similar but longer shafts set into round-arched recesses at the lower stage.

Tall angle buttresses help support the towers and transepts; these are of bold projection, diminishing in stages, and terminating in a sloping set-off. Shorter buttresses are set along the nave and around the apse, and at the clerestory level. The ornate buttresses of the Decorated Period with their crocketed canopies and niches have yet to come, not to mention flying buttresses spanning great arches.

The interior of the Cathedral consists of an aisled nave, very short transepts, and an apsidal choir of French form, with a semi-circular ambulatory running around the sanctuary. With the ambulatory, sanctuary, and choir occupying one half of the total floor space, the nave looks quite small.

West Front Doorway

One is particularly struck by the sense of architectural unity achieved by the network of sturdy vertical shafts and horizontal string courses that frame the bays of both nave and apse – a unity enhanced by the use of circular columns, foliated capitals and chamfered abaci under 'triangular' moulded arches at both the nave and triforium levels. The nave columns are of Bath stone, and red Cork marble is used in the aisle walls up to window level.

Separated from the nave by a wall of white veined marble, the choir is entered through polished brass gates, and a fine brass rail separates the sanctuary from the choir. Beneath the hinged seats of the Canons and Dignitaries (the rear row of each side of the choir stalls) are misericords carved with figures of small animals, insects, and birds.

There is a special concentration of colourful decorative work in the choir and sanctuary areas which stands out in contrast to the stark white limestone of the exterior. A magnificent painting of the choir ceiling dating from 1935 shows Christ in glory surrounded by adoring angels. Below this the mosaic pavement of the sanctuary floor is made of marble from the French Pyrenees, shaped into a detailed illustration of the biblical passage likening the kingdom of Heaven to a net cast into the sea which gathers fish of every kind. Various representative figures from king to slave are caught in the meshes of the net.

The stained glass windows present the Bible story sequentially, commencing with the Creation in the west rose window and continuing around the nave and ambulatory.

Perhaps more than anywhere else, the furnishings of St Fin Barre's provide a special attraction for the visitor. The altar table is of magnificently carved oak, supported on eleven pillars and resting on a plinth of polished black marble. Fittingly enough, it is in memory of John Gregg, Bishop of Cork, who had laid the foundation stone of St Fin Barre's in 1865, and the topmost stones of the two western towers and spires in 1878, just one month before his death. The bishop's throne, also erected to his memory, is set on a plinth of red Cork marble from which it rises to a height of 46feet (14m). Panels enclosing the seat are carved with profiles of 20 of the more illustrious bishops, from St Fin Barre to John Gregg, who have occupied the see of Cork. Elaborate oak carvings are carried up to the crocketed spire of the throne.

The circular stone pulpit resembles a drum. It is supported on a central column of red marble surrounded by four square pillars also of this material. In 1933, the carved figures of the four Evangelists and St Paul around the body of the pulpit were painted over in bright colours.

If the good wine is to be kept till last, it must be the incomparable solid brass lectern that was originally designed by the architect Burges for a cathedral at Lille in France. Ten feet (3m) in height and weighing over 900lb (400k), it stands on a pedestal in the shape of a truncated pyramid supported by four lion paws. The pillar resting on this base has a ring-shaped moulding at its centre set around with rock crystals and ornamented with clusters of fruit and foliage, and the cap at the top of the pillar is also set around with upwards of 50

The Lectern

crystals. The revolving triangular reading desk has profiles of
Moses and David on the side panels, and five candle holders
in rich decorative settings.

St Fin Barre is the patron saint of Cork. He founded a hermitage at Gougane Barra in West Cork in the late sixth century. His greatest work, however, was the foundation of a monastery on the site of the present Cathedral in Cork City, where some evidence of an early Romanesque church and Round Tower has been found.

Location: Bishop Street. Open daily and for Church of Ireland Services.

ST BRENDAN'S CATHEDRAL
Loughrea, County Galway

During the latter half of the nineteenth century, political Ireland was involved with a Land League and Home Rule movement aimed at recovery of land ownership and a measure of self-rule for Catholics. Towards the century's end an offshoot of this endeavour was the Celtic Revival, a movement whose goal was the renaissance of a true Irish cultural identity and the promotion of work by Irish artists. Some scattered attempts to revive also an Irish Romanesque church architecture – Newport Church in Mayo, the Honan Chapel in Cork, and the Church of the Four Masters in Donegal town are examples – were at best a qualified success. The Catholic Cathedral in Sligo town, a worthy edifice predating the Celtic Revival by about 30 years, is the only nineteenth-century example of Romanesque Revival at the cathedral level.

The building of St Brendan's Cathedral from 1897 to 1902 coincided with the beginnings of this Celtic Revival. Architecturally it adheres to the prevailing neo-Gothic pattern. It was designed on a modest scale by the Dublin architect William H. Byrne (1866-1917), with an aisled nave, apsidal sanctuary, unusually shallow transepts, and north-west tower and broach spire. After being largely replaced by the parapet spire of the Decorated period, the broach spire was reinstated as part of the nineteenth-century Gothic revival, often in the company of lucarnes that looked towards the cardinal points.

The glory of the Cathedral is in the interior, in the combination of the creations of some of the best Irish artists and craftspeople expressed through the media of sculpture, stained glass, metalwork, and woodcarving. Much of the inspiration was due to the Loughrea-born Edward Martyn, one of the most dedicated promoters of the Revival.

The main sculptural component is the work of Michael

Shortall, an outstanding student at the Metropolitan School of Art, a late nineteenth-century development from the Dublin Society Schools. Shortall's contributions are the 16 corbels along the clerestory, the two at the sanctuary entrance, the capitals in the transepts and along the nave arcade, the altar with its six-bay marble Romanesque arcade, and the altar rail with interlacings and suggestions of the Celtic High Cross. The 16 carved corbels high up in the clerestory retell the story of the Creation with animals, fish, birds, and foliage. Medieval Irish Romanesque carvings are the models here. Even more impressive are the capitals that crown the polished granite pillars of the nave arcade. Romanesque carvings are again the models in the superb depiction of events in the life and legendary voyage to America of St Brendan the Navigator. A chart listing the subjects is posted at the rear of the church. There are four subjects per capital, and the canvasses are sensibly large enough for effortless viewing. Shortall had been sent to do the work in Loughrea on the recommendation of his teacher, John Hughes R.H.A.(1865-1941), the leading Irish sculptor of his day. Hughes' own contribution was the reredos of the high altar, a bronze piece depicting Christ, the Man of Sorrows. The marble statue of the Virgin and Child on one side altar is also by Hughes – a work of rare beauty and among the finest adornments of the Church.

In 1903 a studio called An Túr Gloine (un toor glih-neh), The Tower of Glass, was opened by Sarah Purser (1848-1943), a respected portrait painter, for the training of artists in the making of stained glass. Its first manager was Alfred Ernest Child of the English Arts and Crafts movement in London. Over the next 50 years, most of the stained glass windows in St Brendan's were the work of several artists of An Túr Gloine. Eight are by Child himself, and six by the distinguished artist Michael Healy (1873-1941), including the Ascension and Last Judgment windows in the south transept, which are among the great modern works in this medium. Healy, a native of Dublin who also studied in Italy, was a member of the Túr Gloine with which he stayed until his

Interior of St Brendan's

death. Here again a directory of the subjects and artists is
prominently posted in the Church. The Stations of the Cross
in mosaic – opus sectile – are by yet another member of An

Túr Gloine, Mary Ethyl Rhind. The inscriptions are in Irish.

Edward Martyn's own architect, William A. Scott, was commissioned to design the furnishings. The wrought iron railings that run the length of the Church between the nave and aisles are the work of Scott, as are the eye-catching lamp standards set under the arches of the nave arcade.

In 1902 the Celtic Revival was further advanced by the establishment of the Dun Emer Guild, a co-operative which provided the Cathedral with a set of 24 colourful sodality banners woven in silk and wool on linen, also with inscriptions in Irish. The designs were provided by the well-known painter, Jack B. Yeats. No longer used in the Church, the banners are displayed along with other liturgical items of historic interest in the nearby diocesan museum.

In compliance with Vatican II requirements, new wood furnishings – altar, ambo, and bench – were designed by the church artist, Ray Carroll. And to the credit of those involved, no existing arrangements were altered. The old altar table still rests on its marble Romanesque arcade, and the Communion rail with its Celtic crosses, interlacings, and bronze angels remains in place.

Location: Loughrea. Open daily.

ST EUNAN'S CATHEDRAL
Letterkenny, County Donegal

St Adhamhnán (oo-nawn) wrote a famous *Vita Columbani*, thereby connecting his name with that of Ireland's second most beloved saint. Columba (Colmcille) was born in Gartan, County Donegal, in 521. Before going into exile to Iona in Scotland, he had founded monasteries in Derry, Kells, and Durrow. Eunan (624-704), a native of Raphoe, also in County Donegal, became ninth Abbot of Iona in 679. In that capacity, countering the violence of the times, he championed the cause of women and children in a book called *The Law of the Innocents*.

Architecturally speaking, it is hardly incorrect to describe St Eunan's as the last of the ambitious Catholic neo-Gothic cathedrals of the nineteenth century. The contemporary Loughrea Cathedral is technically Gothic but altogether Celtic Revival in spirit. Completion of Cobh Cathedral in 1914 then marked the end of the road for Gothic Revival as the accepted Irish cathedral style. Of the three Catholic cathedrals built in this century, Mullingar and Galway are ponderous buildings that do not clearly reflect any of the older styles. Cavan Cathedral made a courageous about-face to a brilliant neo-classical Corinthian facade with frontal tower and spire, all strongly patterned on Francis Johnston's design for St George's Church in Hardwicke Street, Dublin, it in turn being derived from James Gibbs design for the Church of St Martin-in-the-Fields in London.

Such was the continued prestige as a monastic centre of St Columba's own foundation at Derry that, as a compliment, it was passed over as a seat of a bishopric of Donegal in favour of Raphoe at the Synod of Rathbreasail in 1111. Derry did not become a see until 1254. So it was the older Cathedral of St Eunan in the historic diocese of Raphoe that was transferred to the Church of Ireland during the Reformation. Much more recently, however, large size and proximity to Raphoe made

Letterkenny the logical choice for the siting of the magnificent Cathedral of Saints Eunan and Columba that now occupies a spectacular position overlooking the town. It was begun in 1891 and completed in 1901.

The style is late thirteenth-century French Gothic, where the delicacy and lightness of the Gothic ideal are realised in the graceful lines and proportions of the smooth sandstone exterior. Against traditional practice, the nature of the site necessitated a west rather than east positioning of the sanctuary. So the entrance facade is at the east end, and consists of three deeply recessed doorways set between four slim towers braced together by flying buttresses over arcades of cusped arches, the inner, taller towers framing a huge recessed arched window with geometrical tracery. Statues of Saints Eunan and Colmcille are set into canopied niches on each side. The finest feature of the exterior is the almost free-standing tower and spire offset to the southwest, where the decorative touches added to the slim, tapering, octagonal spire are of particular effect (crockets around the peak, and banding with rows of gargoyles further down), decorative effects nicely complemented by the crocketed spirelets over the east end towers and the corner pinnacles of the great south-west tower itself.

Under large wheel windows, the doorways of the north and south transepts are Irish Romanesque in character with semi-circular arches under triangular gables, and finely-carved Celtic interlacing. Within a moulded trefoil in the tympanum of the north doorway is a carving of the Holy Family at work – carpenter's tools for Joseph and a spinning-wheel for Mary. The matching south doorway shows St Patrick preaching to a group of long-haired peasants whose tight-lipped expressions certainly give nothing away.

Within the rather dark interior, wall and ceiling decoration is largely confined to the sanctuary area and its adjacent chapels. Apart from the usual representations of scriptural subjects, the theme of the interior is a celebration of the saints of Donegal, with emphasis on Eunan and Columba. Most demonstrably, the tribute to Saints Eunan and Columba

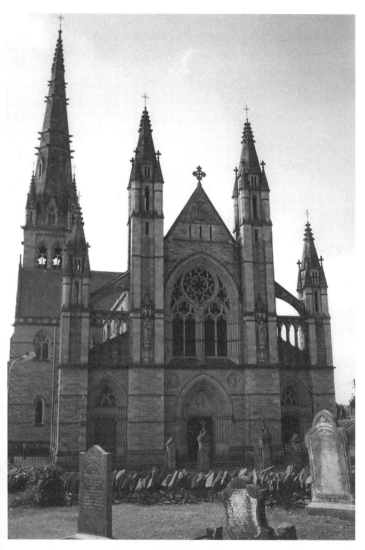

St Eunan's Cathedral

is set out along the metre-wide ribbon of carving that forms a great archway between the nave and crossing, filled with a series of high-relief narrative carved panels separated and bordered by a continuous rope moulding. St Eunan is assigned the south column where he is shown being received as a young novice into Iona, listening to the older monks of Iona narrating the life of Columba, presenting *The Law of the Innocents* at Tara, and as first Bishop of Raphoe. In a celebrated controversy, when Columba copied a psalter without permission of its owner, St Finian, a bloody copyright battle ensued and the saint went into exile to Scotland. In a lower panel on the north side Columba is shown transcribing this manuscript. Proceeding upwards, Columba is shown preaching to a group of Scottish chieftains, speaking for the Irish bards at the Convention of Drumceat in 563 (to stave off a threat of their banishment), and on his deathbed at Iona.

The celebration continues in the Chapel of St Columba, currently the Baptistry, where the altar-piece shows further events in the saint's life, and the painted ceiling by Oreste Amici sets the heads of Donegal saints into a mass of swirling Celtic designs. Carved busts of Donegal saints are placed between the arches of the polygonal sanctuary; the dove on the shoulder of each saint is a mark of his spiritual affinity with Colmcille, the Dove of the Church.

The Gothic ideal is reasserted in the profusion of stained glass in every part of the building. Not to be missed is the memorable Drumceat Rose Window in the north transept, executed in 1910 by Michael Healy, note of whose work in Loughrea Cathedral has already been made. The visitor might also take special note of the ten abstract clerestory windows of Ireland's greatest Symbolist artist, Dublin-born Harry Clarke (1889-1931), whose superb artistry is represented in many churches throughout Ireland, and remembering that the work of Clarke must be *seen* to be appreciated. His masterpeice is the stained glass in the Honan Chapel in University College Cork. The nave windows – from Munich – with male saints on the south wall and female saints opposite, are a reminder of the days when men and women were separated in church.

It was an enlightened decision that left the high altar in its original position after the stipulations of Vatican II. Its altar piece, a copy of Leonardo da Vinci's *Last Supper*, was simply moved forward to the new altar table front, leaving everything else as before. The communion rails and exquisite marble Pulpit of the Four Masters, both by the Dublin firm of Michael Pearse, were thus spared.

Annals from various parts of the country are a main source of information on medieval Irish ecclesiastical history. Among the more important are the *Annals of the Four Masters* compiled in Donegal between 1622 and 1636 by a group of Franciscan monks led by Michael O'Clery. It was fitting that Donegal should give special recognition to these dedicated Franciscan scholars. Statues of the Four Masters (more correctly five) in Italian Carrara marble are set around the perimeter of the pulpit in the company of the Four Evangelists and the prophet Isaiah.

In a brief account such as this it is not possible to do more than draw attention to the salient features of the building. More than one visit is required to view the abundance of detail that makes up this or indeed any other cathedral of note. But each successive visit will reveal new beauties, and reward with new insights.

Location: Letterkenny, overlooking town.

KNOCKANURE CHURCH
Moyvane, County Kerry

The little chapel-of-ease at Knockanure was in the vanguard
of the move towards use of a radically modern architectural
idiom in Irish church design, and has since exerted a powerful
influence in Irish church building. It was designed by Michael
Scott and Partners of Dublin and London, commenced in 1961
and consecrated in 1964. The structure is very simple: flat-
roofed with two load-bearing concrete brick walls for the
sides supporting concrete T-beams at roof level. Transparent
glass frames form the front and rear facades, with the side
walls projecting beyond these in a manner reminiscent of the
antae of early Irish churches. A huge carved wood relief of the
Last Supper by the Irish artist Oisín Kelly acts as a screen
across the entrance. Throughout his life, Oisín Kelly (1915-81)
was a leading artist in the religious field; he worked in stone,
wood and bronze. The building is elevated on a surrounding
podium and approached from the front by a very wide set of
six steps; the impression is of a temple raised above the
surrounding landscape. Horizontal and vertical lines combine
everywhere to create a rigidly symmetrical effect.

The interior of the Church is screened from the sacristy at
the rear by a free-standing white wall that acts as a reredos.
Light is supplied by the glass frames across the front and rear,
and the simple beams set across on top of the side walls allow
light to penetrate beneath the roof covering. The altar of black
limestone on a stepped platform stands out against the stark
whiteness of the wall behind it. It dominates the building and
is the focal point of the interior, and because the Church is
small, an intimate atmosphere is achieved. The only feature
that might be described as just decorative is a small Madonna
and Child mounted on the wall at the side of the altar. Large
artistic tapestries in gold and black, making up the 14 Stations
of the Cross, relieve the bareness of the side walls. The only
other furnishing is the bronze crucifix over the altar by

194

Knockanure Church

the Berlin-born Imogen Stuart, whose art style is distinctively personal. A versatile artist, Stuart also works in wood and stone.

The Catholic Church at Sion Mills, County Tyrone, which was built in 1965, also has a Last Supper frieze by Oisín Kelly above the front entrance – in this and in its general aspect it bears a marked resemblance to Knockanure, and with Knockanure has contributed to acceptance of the modern idiom in church building.

Location: Moyvane, 6m (10km) east of Listowel. Open daily.

ST MICHAEL'S CHURCH
Creeslough, County Donegal

The traditional practice in the Catholic Church was that of the clergy conducting the religious services, with the laity in the role of silent onlookers. Mass was celebrated by a priest with his back to the congregation, at an altar placed against the sanctuary wall, and in an area cordoned off from the main body of the church by an altar rail. Celebrant and worshipper were separated both physically and psychologically.

Quite the wrong approach to corporate worship this, according to the Constitution of the Sacred Liturgy that followed the Second Vatican Council of the 1960s. Instead, the people must join with the officiating clergy in the celebration of the liturgy. The altar, facing the people, must be the focal point of the church, and the physical and psychological barriers to participation must be removed. The church building must be simple and welcoming, and the furnishings artistic and edifying.

Knockanure Church heralded the introduction of the modern idiom in Irish church architecture, along with a move towards simpler church furnishings. By the mid-1960s older churches were being variously modified, and new churches were being consciously designed to meet the *full* requirements of Vatican II, and the scores of churches built since then, while exhibiting a vast diversity of architectural detail, have all adhered to the letter of the new code. It must suffice to illustrate the force of the new message by a brief advertence to just one church.

St Michael's Church in Creeslough was designed by Liam McCormick and Partners of Derry, being opened for worship in 1971. Its fan-shaped exterior walls, finished in white pebble-dash, were an original and unique conception. One wonders about the unusual contours of this exterior until it is realised that the building, with its inward-sloping walls, was designed to blend naturally into the surrounding landscape of

St Michael's Church, Creeslough

gentle soft hills; by so doing the architects have realised to the full the potential of a site ideally set between the mountains and the sea.

But much more than because of its relationship to the background mountain scene, the rationale of the fan is boosted by the way in which it enables all the church seating to radiate from a circular sanctuary set into the central curve of the fan. Every worshipper in Creeslough Church faces an altar raised up on two circular platforms, and, with a seating capacity of less than 500, St Michael's also achieves the atmosphere of a small, intimate theatre. So the plan ensures that, in compliance with the new liturgy, the altar is the focal point of the church, and that there is a feeling of communal participation.

Making here a momentary logical digression – the ideally conforming Catholic church would literally have to go to a full circle, with the altar at its centre. Inevitably it did – at Ballylanders in County Limerick, for example, where the viewing was also enhanced by means of a circular tiered seating plan.

There is more. Under the older jurisdiction, the tabernacle had formed an integral part of the altar. When it was required that the altar itself become the focal point of attention, the question of the judicious relocation of the Blessed Sacrament became an issue. To meet this problem in Creeslough, provision was made for a separate Blessed Sacrament Chapel along the left arm of the fan. However, some of this arrangement has recently been changed, and the Tabernacle has been moved back to a pedestal beside the main altar. Somehow the little side chapel now appears to lack a *raison d'etre*.

Also by the McCormick group is the imaginative design of St Aengus Church at Burt, about 20 miles (33km) from Creeslough. It is situated just below the Iron Age hillfort known as Grianán of Aileach, its circular shape inspired by that of the historic Grianán.

Modern churches like Knockanure, Sion Mills, Creeslough, and Ballylanders, have appeared in all sizes and sometimes startling shapes in urban housing estates and rural areas across Ireland. Their novelty and diversity will continue to provide a fertile subject for comment, but as long as the functional and aesthetic remain well blended, there will always be room for innovation.

Location: Creeslough village below Sheephaven Bay.

GLOSSARY

ABACUS Flat slab forming uppermost part of a capital

AMBULATORY Walkway at the east end of a chancel, usually semi-circular or polygonal in shape

ANTAE Side walls of a church projecting beyond the gables – common in early Irish church building and probably designed to support the barge boards of the roof

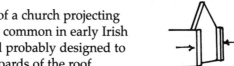

APSE Semi-circular or polygonal extension of the aisles of a church at the altar end

ARCHITRAVE Lowest member in a classical entablature – also moulded frame of window or door

ASHLAR Building stone dressed and squared – used for better finished work

BARREL VAULT Vault (ceiling) usually of stone and semi-circular in shape – also called a *tunnel vault;* called a *pointed barrel vault* if the apex of the vault is pointed

BASILICA Early Christian church derived from Roman hall of justice. Basic plan was a rectangle divided into three aisles by two rows of columns, and having an apse

BATH STONE Honey-coloured limestone quarried at Bath, England

BATTER Inward sloping of wall, doorway, or window

BLIND ARCADE Series of arches along a wall surface – also called a blank arcade

BUTTRESS Projecting masonry mass giving support to a wall. An *angle buttress* (A) is set at each side of a corner. A *flying buttress* (B) transmits the thrust of an inner wall by means of an arch connected to an outer buttress. A *raking buttress* (C) tapers in towards a wall.

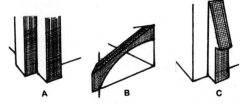

A　　　　　B　　　　　C

CAEN STONE Cream-coloured limestone from Normandy in France. Much used in prestige medieval carving

CANTILEVERED Supported by beams set horizontally into a wall

CAPITAL Top part of column, and frequently ornamented

CASHEL Enclosure surrounded by drystone masonry wall

CELTIC REVIVAL Late nineteenth- and early twentieth-century movement in art and architecture which sought to reintroduce the forms of early Irish Romanesque and to promote work by Irish artists

CHAMFER To bevel off a square corner

CHANCEL East end of a church containing choir (if present) and sanctuary

CHEVRON Inverted V developed into a zigzag ornament of Norman origin – commonest motif in Irish Romanesque art

CHOIR That part of a church where services are sung

CLASSICAL Name given to architecture of Ancient Greece and Rome, and its later derivatives

CLERESTORY Upper storey of the nave walls of a church

CLOCHÁN Stone beehive-shaped hut built using the corbelling technique

COFFERED CEILING Ceiling decorated with sunken panels

CONSOLE BRACKET S-shaped ornamental supporting bracket

CORBELS Projecting stones set along a wall as floor supports

CORINTHIAN Most ornamental Greek Order. Column has shaft and base which may resemble the Ionic. Capital features acanthus-leaf and other foliate design and abacus has foliate ornament in the centre of each face. Entablature frequently richly ornamented.

CORNICE Upper member of a classical entablature – also ornamental moulding around room walls just below ceiling

CROCKET Ornamental scroll-like carving of curved foliage along the upper edge of any sloping surface

CROSSING Space (usually under a tower) in a cruciform church, at the meeting of choir, nave, and transepts

CUSP In curvilinear tracery a projecting point formed by two segments of a circle

DECORATED Second period (fourteenth century) of Gothic style – characterised by elaborate curvilinear window tracery, complex rib vaulting, and use of floral and naturalistic decoration

DENTILS Series of small rectangular projections resembling teeth used for ornamental purposes in classical architecture

DIAPER Repetitive ornamental pattern

DOGTOOTH Thirteenth-century ornament consisting of series of pyramids with indented edges

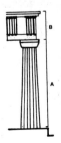

DORIC Oldest Greek Order. Has baseless column (A) with (usually) fluted shafts (flutes separated by sharp edges called *arrises*), cushion-like capital (*echinus*), and square abacus. Entablature (B) has *triglyphs* separated by *metopes* along the frieze. Under each triglyph a row of small ornaments like drops, called *guttae*.

202

Along the soffit of the cornice a row of
rectangular blocks called *mutules*. Guttae
on the undersides of mutules gives the
blocks a domino-like appearance

EARLY ENGLISH Earliest phase
(thirteenth century) of English Gothic, or
Pointed, style – characterised by pointed
arches, lancet windows, geometrical
tracery, and relatively slender articulation

EMBRASURE Wall recess – frequently
splayed

ENGAGED COLUMN Column attached to
wall or other column

ENTABLATURE In classical architecture
the name given to that part of an Order
above the abacus consisting of *architrave*
(A), *frieze (B)*, and *cornice* (C)

ESKER RIADA Ancient name of long
glacial ridge forming a raised east-west
route across Irish midland bog

FILLET Narrow flat band along a
roll-moulding or shaft but sometimes of
V-section – also used between mouldings,
or between the flutes in the shafts of
Classical columns

FINIAL Ornament placed at the apex
of any prominent building feature

FLUTES Vertical concave channels
encircling the shaft of a column in
classical architecture separated by
either a flat band (A) (*fillet*) or a
sharp edge B(B) (*arris*)

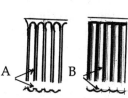

FREESTONE High quality finely-grained sandstone or limestone capable of being chiselled in any direction

FRET Decorative straight-line key pattern

FRIEZE In Classical architecture the middle member of an entablature (between architrave and cornice) – also used to describe any horizontal band of decoration

GARGOYLE Projecting spout used to carry off water from a gutter – frequently carved in the shape of grotesque figures

GOTHIC Austere Early English Gothic architectural style introduced into Ireland *c.*1200. Characteristic features of later Decorated Gothic are pointed or ogee arches, clustered columns, rib-vaulted ceilings, elaborate window tracery, and rich stone carving

GRANGE Outlying farmland and buildings owned by a monastery

GREEK REVIVAL Movement in architecture lasting from about 1760 to 1850 and based on a study of ancient Greek architecture at its source

GROIN VAULT Stone vault produced by the intersection of two barrel vaults – supporting curved ribs along the intersecting lines are called *groin ribs*

HAMMERBEAM Wooden beam projecting horizontally from a wall –

a vertical strut positioned towards
its outer edge helped support the
roof trusses

HEXASTYLE Having six columns

HOOD MOULDING Projecting stone
moulding along the upper part of a door,
arch, or window

IONIC Second Greek Order. Has a
column with base, (usually) fluted
shaft (flutes separated by fillets),
and capital ornamented with spiral-like
projections called *volutes*. Entablature
frequently plain or decorated with rows
of *dentils*

INTERCOLUMNIATION Distance
between columns

LANCET Long narrow window
with lancet (pointed) arch

LINTEL Large flat stone forming the
arch of a doorway

LOZENGE Diamond shape made of
two chevrons

LUCARNE Dormer-like window in a spire
capped by a gable

METOPES Spaces (sometimes decorated)
between triglyphs in a Doric frieze

MISERICORD Hinged seat of choir stall
with shelf fitted to underside – when
turned up, shelf provided support for
clergyman during a long service

MULLION Vertical stone post separating two window lights

NAVE Main part of a church from western entrance to crossing, chancel, or choir

NEO-CLASSICISM Eighteenth-century movement in architecture which sought a return to the pure forms of Classical Antiquity – *Greek Revival* is an aspect of this movement

NICHE Recess in a wall or panel, frequently used as a framework for a statue or carving

NOOK SHAFT Detached shaft set in a corner

OCULUS Small circular (bull's-eye) window – from Latin *oculus*, meaning eye

OGEE ARCH Arch formed of reverse curves much used in Decorated window tracery

ORDER Evolved by the Greeks and employed by the Romans, and determines the disposition, style, proportions, and ornamentation of the columns and entablature in a building – three main Orders are *Doric, Ionic,* and *Corinthian*

PALLADIAN Architecture evolved from the work of Andrea Palladio (1508-80)

PALLIUM Narrow band of white wool with crosses and a pendant strip to front and rear – worn by archbishop as symbol of office

PEDIMENT In Classical architecture a low-pitched triangular gable over a portico, facade, doorway, or window – may also be of *broken-apex* or *broken-base* type

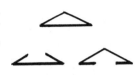

PENDENTIVE Spandrel between lunettes surmounted by dome

PERPENDICULAR Last of the Gothic styles lasting from *c.*1400-1550 – features light mouldings and proportions, lattice-like tracery, and 4-centred arches, square arrangement of mouldings over doorways creating spandrels on the sides

PERPYN WALL Wall of uncoursed rubble about 1.5m high built under the piers and along the length of the nave arcade in a Cistercian church

PILASTER Rectangular pier projecting slightly from a wall

PINNACLE Decorative terminating feature on a parapet or arch often in the form of a turret-like spire

PORTICO Roofed porch usually attached to the front of a building and supported by columns along its front edge (*prostyle*)

PORTLAND STONE Durable and
workable type of limestone

PROSTYLE Having a row of columns
in front of a building

PUT-LOG Rectangular wooden beam
placed in a wall to support scaffolding

QUADRIPARTITE Ribbed vault in which
the ribs are the curved diagonals of two
intersecting pointed barrel vaults –
may be square or rectangular in plan

QUATREFOIL Having 4 lobes –
similarly *trefoil* (having 3 lobes), and
cinque-foiled (having 5 lobes)

QUOINS Dressed stones at the external
angles of a building

REAR-ARCH Arch spanning the innermost
part of a window embrasure

REFECTORY Dining room in a
monastery – also called a *frater*

RENDERING Coating applied to an
exterior wall. Stucco, a smoothly applied
fine lime plaster, a popular rendering
of eighteenth/nineteenth-century Irish
churches

REREDOS Stone or wooden screen behind
a church altar

RIB A raised moulding on a ceiling –
includes (A) *formerets* (vaulting ribs
along meeting place of wall and

ceiling), (B) *tiercerons* (additional decorative ribs that spring from the corners of a vaulting bay), (C) *lièrnes* (subsidiary vaulting ribs set between the main ribs linked to the springing points of the bay)

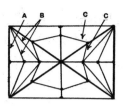

ROLL MOULDING Moulding of semi-circular or more than semicircular section

ROMANESQUE Architectural style prevalent in Ireland *c.*1130-1200, characterised by round arches, solid wall construction, heavy cylindrical piers, flat buttresses. Doorways, windows, and chancel arches frequently decorated with geometrical, human, animal, and floral designs, chevrons predominating

ROOD Crucifix

RUBBLE Coarse walling of roughly-dressed stones – used for wall construction in most early Irish churches and medieval abbeys

RUSTICATION Masonry with joints of square or chamfered (V-shaped) section – blocks are emphasised to give an impression of size and strength

SCALLOPS Semi-circular curves used as an ornamental edging on a capital

SCRIPTORIUM Writing-room in a monastery

SEDILIA Seats on the south side of a chancel for the use of celebrants

SLYPE Passage through east walkway of Cistercian cloister to abbot's house, infirmary and monks' burial ground outside east range

SOFFIT Underside of a lintel or arch

SOUTERRAIN Underground passage used as place of refuge or storage

SPANDREL Space between an arch and the rectangle containing it, or between two adjacent arches

SPIRE Tall thin feature (usually) pyramidal or octagonal shape surmounting a tower – includes (A) *needle spire* (slender spire set well inside the tower top), (B) *broach spire* (octagonal spire set on a square tower with four semi-pyramidal masonry wedges called broaches (b) (at the angles of the tower), (C) *parapet spire* (spire set behind a parapet)

STIFF-LEAF Foliage design featuring mainly stylised trefoil leaves, and characteristic of thirteenth-century Early English Gothic

STOP Termination of a hood-moulding – often ornamented, e.g. with human mask

STRING COURSE Horizontal band of moulding along a wall

SWITCHLINE Tracery produced by the intersection of mullions in the upper part of a window – the lines converge as they rise

TETRASTYLE Portico with four columns

TRACERY Decorative treatment of open stonework above Gothic window mullions. Includes *switchline* (where lancet curves intersect to form lozenges), *reticulated* (like a network or honeycomb), *flamboyant* (flamelike), *geometric* (which uses geometric figures such as circles, trefoils, quatrefoils), *curvilinear* (from Decorated Gothic, using flowing curves and ogee forms), and *panel* (from Perpendicular Gothic, using mainly vertical lines)

TRANSEPTS North and south arms of a cruciform church

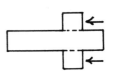

TRANSITIONAL Style of architecture between Romanesque and Gothic which

lasted from about 1160 to 1200, and used features of both styles

TRIFORIUM In a church the arcaded middle storey between the nave and clerestory levels

TRIGLYPHS Three-grooved tablets set between metopes in a Doric frieze

TYMPANUM Space enclosed by a semi-circular arch over a doorway

WATTLE-AND-DAUB Type of wall construction consisting of interwoven branches (wattles) covered with mud (daub) – probably roofed with thatch or marsh reed